ABOUT BRITAIN NO.

THE LAKES TO TYNESIDE

WITH A PORTRAIT BY
SID CHAPLIN

PUBLISHED FOR
THE FESTIVAL OF BRITAIN OFFICE
COLLINS
14 ST JAMES'S PLACE
LONDON

THE **ABOUT BRITAIN** GUIDES

List of Titles

The Relief Maps used for the covers and jackets of these books
were designed and produced by Geographical Projects Ltd.

Produced by A. N. Holden & Co. Ltd., London, and printed in England by Sun Printers Ltd.,
London and Watford. Published by Wm. Collins Sons & Co., Ltd., in 1951.

Roman forts at Chew Green, Northumberland.

CONTENTS

LIST OF PHOTOGRAPHERS

A SHORT READING LIST

Armstrong, A. M., Mawer, A., etc. *Place-names of Cumberland*. Cambridge University Press. 1950. 18s.

Collingwood, G. *Lake District History*. T. Wilson, Kendal. 1925. 5s.

Collingwood, W. G. *The Lake Counties*. Dent. 1949. 7s. 6d.

Collingwood, R. G. *A Guide to the Roman Wall*. A. Reid, Strawberry House, Newcastle-on-Tyne. 1948. 2s.

Cook, G. H. *Portrait of Durham Cathedral*. Phoenix House. 1948. 12s. 6d.

Honeyman, H. L. *Northumberland*. Robert Hale. 1949. 15s.

Kinvig, R. H. *A History of the Isle of Man*. University of Liverpool Press. 1950.

Nicholson, Norman. *Cumberland and Westmorland*. Robert Hale. 1949. 15s.

Ramsden, D. M. *Teesdale*. Museum Press. 1947. 12s. 6d.

Sharp, Thomas. *Cathedral City*. (Durham) Architectural Press. 1945. 5s.

Sitwell, A. *Northumberland*. Paul Elek. 1948. 10s. 6d.

Thompson, B. L. *The Lake District and the National Trust*. T. Wilson, Kendal. 1946.

Trevelyan, G. M. *The Middle Marches*. A. Reid, Strawberry House, Newcastle-on-Tyne. 1s. 6d.

Details of everything which belongs to the National Trust will be found in the inexpensive *National Trust: List of Properties*, 1950. See also *National Trust Guide: Buildings*, by J. Lees-Milne, 1931 and the *National Trust Guide: Place of Natural Beauty*, by D. M. Matheson, 1950.

MAPS

Excellent maps for the whole of Britain are published by the Ordnance Survey and by Bartholomew. The most useful for travellers are the one-inch and the quarter-inch series. In addition, a series of special maps is published by the Ordnance Survey, each covering Britain in two sheets on the scale of 1/625,000 (about ten miles to one inch). This series includes: 'Coal and Iron'; 'Land Classification'; 'Land Utilisation'; 'Railways'; 'Types of Farming'; 5s. per sheet; and 'Solid Geology' 12s. 6d. per sheet.

The tailpieces used in this book are from wood engravings by the Northumbrian artist Thomas Bewick (1753-1828), who is referred to on page 63.

The Cheviot hills, seen from the slopes of Simonside.

USING THIS BOOK

THIS GUIDE-BOOK is one of a series 'About Britain,' so we hope, in a new way. Like the others (there are thirteen altogether) it contains many photographs, a map, a gazetteer, and illustrated strip-maps of the most convenient itineraries. And it begins with a portrait of the district—an account of many of the facts about it which are worth knowing and many of the things which are worth seeing.

This does not explain the newness. These guides have been prompted by the Festival of Britain. The Festival shows how the British people, with their energy and natural resources, contribute to civilization. So the guide-books as well celebrate a European country alert, ready for the future, and strengthened by a tradition which you can *see* in its remarkable monuments and products of history and even pre-history. If the country includes Birmingham, Glasgow or Belfast, it includes Stonehenge. If it contains Durham Cathedral, it contains coal mines, iron foundries, and the newest of factories devising all the goods of a developing civilization. If it includes remnants of medieval forest, it includes also the new forests of conifers transforming acres of useless land. It contains art galleries and wild scenery, universities and remote villages, great ports and small fishing harbours, shrines of national sentiment and institutes of scientific research—the past and the present. On the Downs in Wiltshire we can stand on a minute plot of ground on which the Iron Age farmer reaped his corn with a sickle, and watch a few yards away a combine harvester steadily devouring ripe acres of wheat.

What we are as a people, where we have our homes, what we do, what we make—cotton in Lancashire, tin plate in South Wales, cars outside Oxford, mustard or clothes in Norwich, woollens in Bradford —depends all of it upon a thousand national peculiarities, of soil, vegetation, minerals, water, ways of transport, the continuity and the accidents of history.

It is this living country of today which these guide-books emphasize, the place and the people, not only the country of the past or the exquisitely varied landscape of fields and moors and mountains and coast. They are handbooks for the explorer. The aim is to show what Britain is now, in the North, the Midlands and the South, in East Anglia and the West, in Wales, Scotland, Northern Ireland, and to explain something of the why and wherefore. To investigate this Britain the sensible explorer has to take to the roads and the by-roads. This accounts for the itineraries and the strip-maps, which have been devised to guide you, if you need them, as simply, quickly and comprehensively as possible through the districts portrayed by word and illustration in each book.

The Festival of Britain belongs to 1951. But we hope these explorers' handbooks will be useful far beyond the Festival year.

THE LAKES TO TYNE-SIDE

A PORTRAIT BY SID CHAPLIN

Keswick : The Bronze Age circle.

ENTER this region by the west or the east (there is no middle road unless you care to walk along mountain ridges), by Lancaster or by Northallerton, and you are conscious at once of a change in the atmosphere. Vision is clearer, shapes are more clearly defined – except when mountain mists or the smoke from blast-furnace and colliery chimney-stacks drift across the line of vision. Speech in the way of business is also more direct, but the dialects change from valley to valley, though all are salted with Scandinavian speech.

It is a complex territory, and it would take a very long sentence to sum it up. Those fond of generalization are apt to dismiss the north-east as mainly industrial because they have seen collieries fringe road and rail; pithead pulleys as regular as the mile-castles along the Roman Wall; or because they have heard of the shipyards of Tyne, Wear and Tees, the great engineering works and chemical factories. The same folk dub Lakeland a holiday resort, forgetting the steel towns of Barrow in Furness and the West Cumberland coalfield. Well, Lakeland has to live when the tourists have gone home, and unlike the hotels the fellside 'heafs' (the hillside pastures) are open all the year round. And the collieries and steelworks of the north-east merely mask but do not throttle the tiny coastal denes, the villages, the market towns that serve farmers as well as miners, the long valleys that send green spears into the broad flanks of wide heather moors. The vast industrial population, the

7

major percentage of the three million inhabitants, is packed into the coastal collecting-boxes. The industrial fortresses and encampments may be overawing, but they are dwarfed by the vast bulk of the Pennine moors and Lakeland fells and the buckled horseshoe of the Cheviots and Kyloes.

The mountains and fells which divide the valleys shape the land and mark its folk. The shipyard worker in Barrow in Furness shares the heritage of the shepherds and statesmen of the fells: the thousands who pour along Gallowgate and Blackett Road to watch football by Newcastle United, share a dialect that was shaped by the men of the Border Marches, spoken by Percy Hotspur and sung by the singers of ballads.

The heights, the ups and downs, the hopes and fells are never far away. The most level entry is by the Plain of York through Northallerton, but even this entry is nothing more or less than an immensely wide pass be-

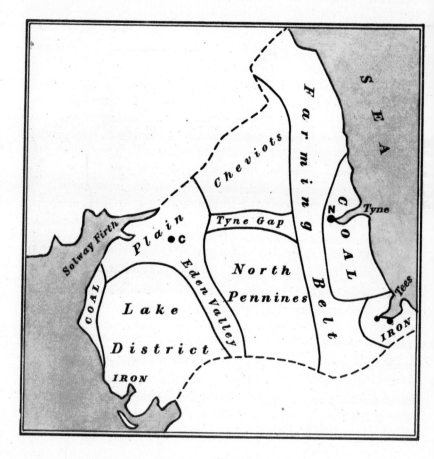

Looking up Wastwater towards Great Gable, Cumberland.

tween the Pennine flanks and the North Yorkshire moors and Cleveland Hills. Life is ordered by the valleys. A man native to these parts is almost bound to have been born in a valley. So he is marked for life with something peculiar which his valley has preserved and passed to him. To describe the whole implies the naming of the parts; naming one by one

A fell farm tucked away under sycamore at Martindale, Ullswater.

the ribs that spring from the bony back and hold all the country together.

To name these valleys is like a splendid roll of the drums which called the men of the dales to the Battle of the Standard, to Neville's Cross and to Otterburn, and to the continual attacks and counter-attacks, raids and reivings of the Border. Wensleydale, Swaledale, Teesdale, Weardale, Tyne, Redesdale and Coquetdale – there is not space to call them all or name the innumerable offshoots. And then west of the steep flank of Cross Fell, the red-sandstone-tinted soil of the Eden Valley; and farther west still, the narrow lake-filled valleys radiating from the central mountain dome of the Lake District. And on the Isle of Man, that clenched fist of rock thrust from the millpond of the Irish Sea, as it appears from Skiddaw, the story is told again in miniature of life in valleys. In Man, too, a language is preserved if not spoken, while the encircling sea has kept intact in all the little valleys a continuity of common law and tradition – a museum of past epochs without the glass cases and with real people.

The fact of communities living between these knuckles of rock gives rise to another unifying feature. The flanks of fells and valleys hide

At Grizedale Park in Lakeland a new forest comes into being.

wealth that a little tunnelling will lay bare – sometimes a mere scratching is sufficient. Wherever you go you are not far from quarries and mines. There was a stone-axe factory at Great Langdale – why not, with such an unlimited supply of stone? Most of the Lakeland farms have their own quarries for road and wall repair. There are great granite and slate quarries. The lakeland fells were worked by Bavarian miners under Queen Elizabeth, and Keswick was once a mining town, with the furnaces going night and day smelting lead ore, carried down the fells on sledges or ponies, and copper ore from Coniston. You may find the tunnel-entrances, dark and narrow and curtained with water dripping from the broken roofs, and little piles of blue copper-sulphate crystals, or crystals of fluorspar, violet on the ground, colourless when held against the sky, or barytes in a confusion of colours, white, yellow, brown, blue and green; all jetsam left by a tide of miners. A great leadmining belt stretches from Hadrian's Wall between Haltwhistle and Corbridge down the Pennine flank to Wensleydale. The Whin Sill has been filleted at points along the length where it is crowned by the Wall; and in most of the dales, there are road-metal and limestone quarries; while the Isle of

Buttermere

Man, until half-a-century ago, was producing lead, zinc, copper and haematitic iron.

Apart from the quarrying, most of this is done with. Only the scars are left and the wind blows desolately through the gaunt barracks set up for the miners. But the leadminers mapped the strata. They were the first practical geologists, not bothering much about fossils, but naming the layers and passing their knowledge, their terminology and above all, their instinct, to the sons and grandsons who left the fells for the coal-fields of Cumberland, Durham and Northumberland.

So to-day it is the coalfields which link the ends of this region. It is astonishing how often and in how many places coal is to be found. The large collieries are in the north-east and run with the Solway shore between Whitehaven and Maryport. But the coal-measures outcrop in the Kyloes and the Cheviots: farms there still have their tall brick chimney-stacks as relics of the day when coal emerged at the very doorstep and every farmer had his own steam-driven threshing-machine. There are out-crops on the Pennine Fells: near Brampton there is a lost little coal-field where they mined 'peacock-coal', almost as hard as anthracite, and where the miners less than a century ago went to Brampton market in dandy wagons pulled by Stephenson's Rocket.

It is to the Tyneside collieries that we owe the modern railway system and the locomotive. Wagonways linked the collieries with the Tyne staithes. First of all wagons were drawn with horses along wooden rails; then iron rails and 'standing' engines were introduced, and then came George Stephenson and Timothy Hackworth who turned wagonway into railway. Both were Tyneside colliery mechanics and both came of mining stock. It was Hackworth who perfected the locomotive and Stephenson who was the first great organizing genius of the railways. When the Stockton and Darlington Railway was opened in 1825 (with Stephenson as engineer), ironstone was found in the Cleveland Hills. So began the growth of Middlesbrough from a farmhouse and a few cottages to what it is at present – a city if judged by size alone. The railway has played its part in the Industrial Revolution, in transforming the country between the Lakes and Tyneside. It even opened the Lakes to the tourist, but it never – it is worth noticing – conquered all of the west coast. If it had, Barrow in Furness with its steel works and shipyards, with its iron works, might have outstripped Middlesbrough in size and

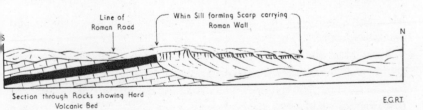

Line of
Roman Road

Whin Sill forming Scarp carrying
Roman Wall

S   N

Section through Rocks showing Hard
Volcanic Bed

E.G.R.T.

The Roman Road and Wall from Newcastle to Carlisle.

13

Packs hitched up: the day begins at a Grasmere Youth Hostel —

even rivalled Newcastle itself. Iron and steel depend on coal, railways depend on coal, so coal, actually and historically, links the whole region in more ways than one. The whole region, that is, except the Isle of Man. This island is not only unique in having cats without tails – it also has the carboniferous limestone without the coal. People have spent time and money looking for it, but up to the moment (the Manx people won't be sorry perhaps) not a knob of coal has been found.

Mining is immensely ancient in our region. The Romans probably raised coal at Benwell (near Newcastle) and may have worked the Northumberland ironstone. But a past does not necessarily mean a future. The mining of lead is almost extinct. Iron-ore mining in Cleveland

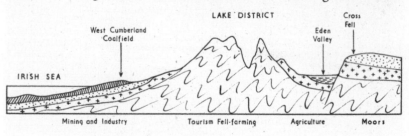

— and a shepherd takes a summer evening stroll over the fells.

and Cleator is a dying industry. The coal-measures are being worked out to the sea. Whether or not atomic energy ever becomes cheaper than coal, the industry is declining, and before so very long all the coal on either side of the Pennines will come from under the sea-bed. There is a great human problem here which the last war submerged but which will become acute again inevitably – the problem of a big population left workless by the decline of a major industry. When the inland pit-heads go to wrack and ruin like the Pennine mine-barracks, and stunted conifers on the waste-heaps struggle to clothe the naked shale, new Trading Estates and factories manufacturing plastic toys, handbags and dresses will not be enough.

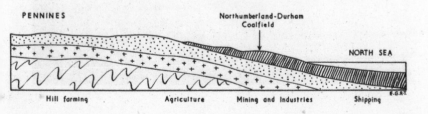

Skiddaw.

Mining in general and coal mining in particular are not the only links that have joined the diverse units of the region. I have mentioned the Scandinavian salting of the dialects. Though the Danes made only limited settlements in Northumberland and Durham they penetrated the North Riding dales, and the Norse, or Norwegian, immigrants settled in Westmorland and Cumberland. The Norsemen possessed themselves of the Isle of Man and founded there the Grandmother of Parliaments – the Tynwald Court, giving it the oldest oral system of law in the British Isles. So this ancestral Scandinavian element is one more link between east and west. And another thing. It was perhaps the Scandinavian homesteaders who first discovered that the best way to deal with the stones gathered from a new 'intake' – that is, land won from the heather and bracken – was to build them into drywalls. The web pattern of drywall (with local variations in technique) is more recent, but it unites the Lakeland dales with the Cross Fell moors, Cross Fell with the Cheviots. The walls are missing only on the Skiddaw-Saddleback group of hills where the nimble-footed Herdwick sheep stick to their own 'heafs' without straying. Otherwise they divide the desolate moors, checker the fells, march with the roads and rivers and hang like necklaces round the high mountains. At High Cup Nick, near Dufton in the Eden Valley, there is a wall that climbs an almost perpendicular cliff of rotten scree. The drywallers worked in all weathers for a few coppers a day. They worked with the material that lay near at hand, ranging in size from small boulders to large pebbles; and gravity was their only cement. The best tribute that can be paid to their craftsmanship is that their walls *belong*. It is as if the very rocks had taken life and sent out stone shoots along with the heather, the bracken, the foxglove and the juniper.

THE SHIFTING SHAPES OF MOUNTAINS

There are as many Lakelands as there are pairs of eyes to see. The mountains and lakes succeed where even saints have failed: they are all things to all men. Tricks of the atmosphere, tantrums of the weather, shifting of vantage points and the range of individual vision all conspire to this end. The packing of so complex a pattern of hills and meres into what is a relatively small area has a deal more to do with it. I remember starting a rare old argument among some farm lads near Bothel when I pointed to a distant peak and asked if it was Skiddaw. The upshot of the argument was that they *thought* it was; so did I, but I'm not sure to

At the Grasmere sports: a team of runners start up Butter Crag —

this day that it was. At a distance the Lakeland mountains are elusive monsters. I know men who have gone year after year to walk the fells and climb the crags and admit their inability to name the mountains. Gable for instance possesses as many faces as a quick-change artist.

But the mountains are all things to all men inwardly as well as outwardly. Wordsworth made them the temple of his religion, Ruskin found inspiration in them, generation after generation of climbers have found a narrow intense joy on the face-climbs. I know an educationalist who says that child delinquents should spend a year living on Helvellyn or Scafell.

In spite of its masses, it is a shifting world. The roof is very near, with clouds skipping along the valley ridges like shapeless sheep. But there is no feeling of imprisonment, as there is in the valleys of South Wales, when the mist thickens from a gauze scarf wrapped lightly round the necks of the hills to a thick grey blanket slung from horizon to horizon. The valleys are wide enough not to be prisons, but not too wide. They remain cosy and homely. They do not produce fighters and rebels but

— and the heavyweight wrestlers come down.

gatherers of flocks, statesmen and homesteaders. Remember that in these valleys the Norsemen forgot their boats and followed sheep instead of plunder.

The fells can be uncomfortable, but never the valley bottoms. And to see the valleys it's of no use to do 'Fourteen Lakes in a Day.' You must use your legs and climb, look down on the mellow landscape and see for yourself rockface melting into scree cliffs, scree to grassy bank, the foliage of cherry and rowan reflected in the lake with the shifting picture of the mountain above in the water below. And over the water, and all around, other mountains and the pattern of drywall, heaf and homestead. And there is more than such views to reward you. There are the mountain gardens in summer, the powdering of lichen on the rocks; foxgloves, harebells, saxifrages, parsley fern and moss-campion; and little orchards where you can fill your handkerchief with bilberry, cowberry, bog whortleberry and stone bramble.

But to return to the view. The prevailing winds of Lakeland are westerly and bring moisture from the sea – small particles suspended in the air – which make a film between the eye and the object. It sometimes produces a sunlight which is white rather than golden, or you can say that the sunlight takes on the magical quality of an infinitely more powerful moon. When that film is absent, as it is on rare occasions, the range and quality of vision is increased a hundredfold and the sky is like a great white diamond with light falling in reversed fountains to splash from the amphitheatre of the hills.

The geological story of how the mountains and lakes came into being and are even now changing is a very wonderful one. The Skiddaw Slates are the oldest rocks. They are mud-rocks, laid by a great sea, and they occupy the great central hump of the lake district, occupying most of the north of the area. Skiddaw itself, Saddleback, the Newlands fells, Grasmoor, Grizedale Pike and the fells about Whinlatter Pass are the Skiddaw Slate masses. Of the lakes, Bassenthwaite, Crummock and Loweswater lie almost entirely in the slate. The slate mountains are rounded with grassy slopes as smooth as sealskin, and they don't often break into crags.

After the mud-rocks, the volcanic. These are the Borrowdale volcanic series. Scafell, the Coniston and Wetherlam fells, the Langdales, the Helvellyn range and the High Street range with most of the central fells are all volcanic. The valleys include Borrowdale, Wasdale, upper Eskdale, Dunnerdale, Mardale and upper Patterdale, but of the larger lakes

Climber on Maiden Moor.

only Haweswater and Thirlmere lie entirely in volcanic rock. Going over Honister Pass (unless you happen to be driving) you can see the bright green shelves of slate in the beck that flows into Buttermere – these are volcanic slates. The volcanoes laid alternate layers of lava and ashes: you can always tell when you are passing these by the terraced effect. The volcanic rock-faces can be as hard and as cold as iron, and some of the screes can wear through shoe-leather in a single afternoon.

South of Coniston are the Silurian rocks, formed, like the Skiddaw slates, in a sea-delta. These southern hills are seldom high, and the fells at night can be the desolate humps of a moon-landscape without the rings. But this is illusion. By the clear light of day they are tender and well-wooded: they are the gentle southland of the Lakes, merging into the ordinary Lancashire landscape. And the main lakes, Coniston and Windermere, are big but unexciting – tempting the motor coaches to stop. If you have known the world Beatrix Potter created in her children's books, you can rediscover her delicate colours in the woods by Coniston, and you can search out her old home at Tilberthwaite farm. But the most exciting thing that can happen to you here is to hire a boat and a rod. You might find a school of perch, and while you're busily pulling them in, a sudden squall might fling the boat and frighten the wits out of you.

These, then, are the main rocks. There are others. The Coniston limestone, Shap granite (you tread on it in the quiet mews of Mayfair or Belgravia), the mountain limestone which gives the Eden valley escarpment of the Pennines the look of a huge white marquee, so that you look for ropes and pegs. And the clean limestone country of the coast, running from Morecambe Bay to the West Cumberland coalfield, giving the iron of Cleator and the coal of Solway. Then comes the red sandstone, colouring the churches, giving the ploughed fields of the Eden valley and Carlisle plain the appearance of raw open strips of flesh in wet weather and the whole countryside a warm glow. And giving the seabirds of St Bees a sanctuary.

If you wish to know more about the rocks, buy a text-book and do your exploring with it stuffed in your pocket. But there is a better way. Climb (within your personal limitations) and feel the rocks underfoot. Handle the sandstone and know the warmth of it as opposed to the reptilian coldness of the Skiddaw slates, a coldness inherited from that delta snake-mother. Walk among the standing stones at Castlerigg or lean your body against the tall stone body of Long Meg. Or climb Wasdale

The huntsman and his hounds listening along
the stone wall for the music of the main pack.

and feel the solidity of bare rock on the summit, the intensity of light. Or skid down to the lake, setting in motion the rotten volcanic screes.

But don't let the masses of mountains, the stretches of water overawe you. Don't be hypnotized by the mountain-idea. Only the sentimental outsider worships mountains: the wide-eyed stone-struck crowd who have followed in the footsteps of Thomas Gray. The sensible man will have no part with this. He will see the mountains and lakes in perspective – with man and beast, tree and plant in the foreground. He will look to the falls of Lodore, but he will also see the Herdwick sheep pouring through narrow gullets of stone as the beck flows through the ghylls. He will see the rocks at a distance and feel the texture of them at close quarters; but he will also see men wrestling in those annual trials of strength which may have come down from the Norsemen. He may smile when first he sees the two locked figures in long pants and stockinged feet, then he will see that this is a slow, deliberate stately dance of strength, men embraced, like rocks in motion, until the ritual ends with the swift untangling of a fall. He will watch the hound-trailing, the sheep-dogs at work, the Lakeland packs setting out. He will keep his ears open for the sound of a kitten mewing in the clouds and when he hears look for the great wing-span of the buzzard. He will hope to see the red deer at Martindale or on Helvellyn. He will listen for the echo of the saga in the voice of shepherd, miner and quarryman.

He will remember that there is more to lakeland than mountain and lake. There is the great circle of castles and peel towers; market towns and centres for selling of cattle and sheep and horseflesh, like Penrith, Appleby, Brough, Kirkby Stephen, Kirkby Lonsdale, Kendal and Cockermouth. There is the coast with its mud-flats and sandy estuaries, the gulleries at Ravenglass and Walney Island. There are the shipbuilders and steelworkers of Barrow in Furness. Beyond St Bees Head the old crumbling castellated collieries stand side by side with concrete and steel pitheads. Two miles out, and three hundred fathoms below the sea-bed men are loading coal. This is the country which bred the American naval officer John Paul Jones and rued it when he returned to Whitehaven in 1778 and spiked the guns in the two forts of the harbour; and it is the country of rum-butter. Will Ritson the champion liar may be dead, but his spirit lives on in the tellers of tall tales in the quayside pubs at Whitehaven and Maryport. And so beyond the true Lakeland where the mountains may be out of mind but not of sight, to Wigton, where they weave John Peel tweed; Carlisle where they make biscuits, and where the sound of Lowland Scots reminds you that the Wall is only a stone's throw away, and of Kinmont Willie riding back home through the border hills with his rescuers.

This, more than any other part of England excepting for Man, is a kingdom apart. The Palatinate of Durham, whose bishop was named a prince and led his armies and minted his own coin, could once lay legal claim to the title. But Lakeland is a kingdom still. Norse blood may have something to do with it, but inaccessibility has had more. The early eighteenth century trail-blazers for the tourist knew Borrowdale, Patterdale and Windermere, but the western valleys were unknown.

The Highlanders of the '45 were able to escape because of the badness of the roads, and even to this day an inadequate road and railway system is a drawback in the industrial west. To this incident we owe the Newcastle-Carlisle road built early in the eighteenth century by General Wade along the ruins of the Wall for part of its distance. George Fox made many converts, and looked upon the district as a haven: Judge Fell may have sheltered him but the remoteness of Lakeland was a factor. John Wesley travelled through the western fells and found the dalemen reluctant to help him – the smuggling that went on at this time may have had a deal to do with their attitude, but no doubt the strong insularity which has kept so much of the past alive also contributed. Like Tyneside the district went on making its songs long after the rest of England had forgotten to sing, and there was a period of native dialect songs following the decline of the ballad. It is a pity these songs are sung no longer, but the Denwoods and others still write strong-timbered dialect verse, and Norman Nicholson, born and bred between the estuaries and the fells, has put the spirit of both in verse that flows through the obscurer crags of contemporary poetry like one of his own mountain becks.

So heights and bad roads and native tradition together have kept this a kingdom to this day; a kingdom which is just as strong on its perimeter as it is in the centre – perhaps stronger; a tradition that lives in the shipyards and at the coalface just as strongly as it does on the fellside or at the quarryface. I would not exchange one mountain for a shepherd or a miner. And it is as well to remember this when controversy arises about reafforestation or hydro-electric schemes. The life of the valleys is too precious to spoil for a view – accepting that the view *is* going to be spoiled. Cheap electricity, good roads, another industry – these are factors which will strengthen the native life unless it is to be cheapened and

Peat diggings on the Cumberland coast

thinned for the traffic in tourists and holiday-makers. This native life, with its rich dialect, customs and tradition is of more value than mountain views. But my faith in this environment is that it will take the plantations and the dams as it has already taken the drywalls, mines and quarries and reservoirs, and merge them with itself. A landscape that was laid down by seas, thrown up by volcanoes, fashioned by the shivering of the strata and sculpted by the great glaciers can surely laugh at trees and concrete and pygmy pylons.

THE ISLE OF MAN

When the Norsemen invaded the Lakes they had already established themselves in Ireland and made a possession and base of the Isle of Man. Only a little larger than England's smallest county – Rutland – Man is a treasure house of history, legend and tradition. Looking at it from Blackpool it is a mere mountain mass projecting from the Irish Sea

Then, approaching it in a boat, one sees the long, low strip projecting like a tongue from the lip of the mountains. That is Point of Ayre. And southwards there is the short stub of lowland that is Langness and the country around Castletown. In the latter town the famous Manx clipper-built vessel the 'Peggy' is still preserved, last of a famous line.

The Manx have always been a sea-faring people, and no doubt the tradition will continue, although the fishing industry has declined. There is a story that the Island gets its name from Manannan, legendary pilot, merchant and magician who could at will hide himself in a mist – and to this day the first view of the island as you approach is of the peaks and hogsback line of the mountains enveloped in a similar cloak. The sign of the Three Legs may have been brought from the Mediterranean by a Scandinavian King; a Manx captain won Nelson's favour; and the English coastline was familiar with the small, fast Manx boats designed for the 'trade' – smuggling. And curiously enough three of the men prominent in the Bounty mutiny had Manx connections – Bligh married a Manx girl, Fletcher Christian was of Manx blood, and Peter Heywood was pure Manx.

Is it to be wondered that the Manx make good sailors? The central mountains are stone sails against which the prevailing south-westerly winds beat unendingly. The dwarf ash trees crouch on the bare slopes, cringing from the wind. The great winds, the gales off the sea, are personified in the Biggane, the Manx giants whose joy and delight it is to uproot trees and unroof buildings. There is a tale of St Trinian's Church being unroofed time and time again, until at last in despair it was left without one. These giants shout on stormy nights, but some say that their voices are merely the gales making trumpets of the glens or of hollows in the crags. There is, too, the Cughtagh, a sea-monster dwelling in the caves of the cliffs or the chasms of Cregneish. His voice rises with the storms and the racing of the tides. The sea is very near the Manx, it is a constant challenge. And when times were hard, the land yielding little, or when the Lords of Man demanded too much, the sea was a way of escape.

In spite of the crowds at Ramsey and Douglas, in spite of the cheerful gorse in the Manx glens, there is an element of melancholy about Man. The coastal holiday towns are gay and prosperous, but inland, as you walk through the glens you see the empty cottages, the tholtans, left when hundreds of Manxmen had to emigrate in the late eighteenth and early nineteenth centuries. For, however much one may feel inclined to blame the holiday resorts for draining away the life of the glens, it is not really true to the facts. The holiday trade came long after the damage was done. Man has been neglected by the social historians. Where the other Celtic nations have managed to preserve their language and culture the Manx have failed, and when the question is asked *why* there is no answer. But how devastating the breakdown was can be seen in the decline of the language – which is allied to the Highland Gaelic and to Irish. In 1730 over two-thirds of the population spoke Manx and Manx alone. Now it is a dead language, reserved only for the opening of Tynwald, with odd words and phrases surviving in common speech.

If Man is a treasure house, it is a treasure house of the dead and of the past. The Manx have a very real reverence for the dead and for the monuments they left. There are more undisturbed stone circles and prehistoric burial places to the square mile than any other district in the British Isles.

But it is the early Celtic era which gave the Island its most wonderful monuments. Before the Christian crosses with their twist and plait carvings and sculptured 'strip cartoons' - if one may dare to use this term for such elemental pictorial art – there were the Ogham stones, carved with the runes of that curious alphabet. Of the Celtic Christian crosses, one of the most remarkable – and it is only a fragment – was found on the Calf of Man. The robed figure of Christ is nailed to the cross. The Body does not hang: it is solid, massive, erect with the cross. The face is bearded and moustached, the eyes heavy-lidded. The nails piercing the hands and feet are large-headed and round. The robes and ornaments are those of a Celtic bishop, while the Roman soldier wears what was probably the dress of a Celtic warrior. He is a mannikin, an evil caricature with huge chin and grotesque nose, dwarfed by the huge figure whose side he will soon pierce.

You should see also the Odin Cross of Kirk Andrea which unites Celtic art with Scandinavian mythology and the Christian faith. On one side a naked angular Odin thrusts his spear into the breast of a leaping wolf while the raven crouched on his shoulder seems to whisper the end of all things. On the other side is depicted the Christian victory over the old faith.

Many rulers and many changes have come to Man since these crosses were hewn and carved. The Manx have survived all, assimilating when they liked, silently rejecting what they did not desire. They are a silent, uncommunicative race, except for their love of singing which they

In the Vickers-Armstrong shipyards at Barrow in Furness.

share with the other Celtic nations. They may survive this last conquest of kindness and prosperity. The things they do not talk about – a recent writer has praised the lack of rabid nationalism among them – they may still hold to in their hearts. In the meantime the past of the kingdom is more alive, more vital, than its present.

In case this may sound as prejudiced criticism, let it be said that Man possesses lovely mountain and coastal scenery. It has been well said that from Snaefell on a clear day can be seen six kingdoms, England, Ireland, Scotland, Wales, Man itself and the Kingdom of Heaven. To some it would appear that the two latter find a meeting place in the unspoilt interior. And it must be an interesting if salutary experience to come down from the raw mountains and quiet glens some day to the smell of petrol and the whine of high-powered engines as one of the annual tourist trophy or motor-cycle races takes place.

WENSLEYDALE CHEESE AND CLEVELAND IRON

You can measure your miles and mark boundaries in this region by

The river at Wearhead in Durham.

the changing breeds of sheep. Only on the Isle of Man has the native breed declined to one last flock – the Loghtan, with reddish brown wool and (in the male) four curled horns; narrow high-backed and goatlike. But in Lakeland the native breed of Herdwicks still abound, small, black-faced, more than competent climbers and amazing jumpers. In the Cheviots and Kyloes you find the Border Leicesters, the black-faced mountain sheep and the native Cheviots. And Wensleydale and Swaledale have also their native breeds, the former blue-faced with long curly fleece, the latter black-faced with –

> Back like a brig,
> Tail like a lonk,
> Horns like a sickle,
> Eyes like a weasel.

I do not know of any Cleveland breed, but there they have their own horse, the Cleveland Bay, splendid at County shows, bred for pulling and ploughing through the clayey Cleveland fields, and cross-bred with thoroughbreds for hard hunting over the hills.

Pendragon Castle commands the pass over to Wensleydale. How or

Salmon-fishing on the south Tyne at Featherstone Bridge, Northumberland.

why it got its name no one knows. It is locally said to have been connected with the father of King Arthur, but it is a Norman building, refashioned by the Lady Anne Clifford, that great lady whose name (as I have said) still lives, not for the castles and churches she rebuilt, but for her good deeds, in the mouths of the common folk. Pendragon marks for me the end of Lakeland. You are passing through the Mallerstang valley-pass. The river is still with you but soon it turns to its main feeder in Hell Gill Beck and you are going down the road to Garsdale at the head of Wensleydale. The fell rises immensely around you. There are no crags or peaks, only great curves running up to meet the sky and the solitary wastes of bent grass and bogs. The white road dances like an unrolling tape. There is a breadth about this bare opening to the most comfortable of the western Pennine dales, but the breadth is bleak and wild. To be alone on the stretches of parched bent and bracken in high summer can be a terrifying business, especially if you are not sure of your bearings. Yet fortunes have been made, families founded, between these wide fells. The farmers of Gasdale, Dent and Hawes were more akin to the statesmen of Cumberland and Westmorland than their Yorkshire

Northumberland coast at Seahouses.

neighbours. They kept sheep, mined lead, quarried marble and built woollen mills. But they went out with knee-breeches, when the long knitted stockings were no longer needed, when the big mills of Lancashire and rising industrialism took away their trade, and the farms were sold out to be rented to strangers.

The great fells rise on either side in terraces to rock-face outcrops like thrones, white in the noonday sun. Over the tops the sea of ling and heather rolls to Swaledale with tumbling ling-thatched mine-shops beside lonely becks. You can trace the fallen levels till they dip to the vein. Into these the miners walked, knitting as they went, knitting as they rested for the space of a 'few needles'.

But farther down are the rich meadows and pastures and the market towns, Hawes in the upper dale, Leyburn in the lower. Here you feel on safe ground. You may eat the mild cheese which the monks of Jervaux have left as a memorial more enduring than the walls of their abbey. Middleham-trained horses may be the best in the land, but Wensleydale cheese is one of the glories of England, and if you can find a table that

Guillemots on the rocky pinnacles of Staple Island, in the Farne Islands.

will provide the best native fare it will pay you not to move on for a
night or two. You can come straight from the glory of the great lakes
to sit beside Semmerwater, that gem of the small lakes; or go up to
Buttertubs and see the water disappear into the deep clefts; hear the
forest horn blown at Bainbridge and walk beside that stretch of the
River Ure between Aysgarth and Redmire where it becomes a series
of cataracts, a parade of leaping water.

Richmond is the gateway to the sister dale of Swaledale. But it is not
counted part of it, neither is it akin to Swaledale settlements like Reeth,
Muker and Keld. It has shared in the wealth of the fells, but it has main-
tained its detachment from the more naked life of the shepherds and
miners. No doubt its traditional position as a garrison town has helped
towards this. Edmund Kean acted in the little eighteenth-century
theatre in Friar's Wynd and one can see him walking through the streets
of tall Georgian houses to a rehearsal. But one cannot by any stretch of
the imagination see him among the laconic miners of Gunnerside. The
clicking of needles would have unnerved him in any case. Richmond is

33

urbane and friendly, a world-wise town with wynds and courts radiating from the cobbled market place; overshadowed by the castle, which stands on a rock almost encircled by the river. Whether by accident or design, Richmond has form at a distance, and at close quarters it retains it. If ever large-scale development had reached the lead mines it might have lost this shapeliness; as it is, apart and aloof from the main stream of traffic, the shapeliness remains. The old church in the market place is arcaded in the Italian manner with little shops around it, and every evening the curfew is rung; the gasworks are out of sight, and, best of all the good gifts that Richmond has to offer, the little teashops are hospitable with a good cup of tea and hot buttered scones. There are no snack bars in Richmond: one advantage of not being situated on the Great North Road.

At Grinton, where Swaledale proper begins – 'From Hollow Mill Cross to Stollerstone Stile, The extent of Swaledale is twenty long mile' – you might be in another world. Here was the end of the Corpse Way which ran from the upper dales to the one church. The poor who wished to bury their dead in consecrated ground carried the coffin over this long painful road, and there are stones to mark where they stopped for a rest. Between Muker and Reeth was the great lead-mining area, between the fork of Swaledale and Arkengarthdale. Go up to Arkengarthdale and level mouths and ruined mine buildings litter the roadside. But you must follow the fading miners' tracks across the fells to find the Swaledale mines, some of them so remote that the miners took a week's provisions with them and slept in the mine shops. Spanish lead and failing veins brought about the final depression. Sometimes an entire street stands empty. There was a boom in the cotton industry at the time and the Lancashire mill owners sent horse-drawn vans to transport furniture and families over the Pennines. Others went abroad, some went to the coalfields. In Durham homes you may often see faded photographs of scenes in Arkengarthdale, Muker, Keld, Reeth. And I have heard tales of the confusion of the lead miners at the coalface when confronted with horizontal instead of vertical working, coal instead of ore, strange tools and new words.

In Arkengarthdale some of the huge smelt mills are still standing. They are built on the scale of castles like Bolton and Middleham, as if their builders had taken an example from them. It is said that when one of the mills was pulled down there was enough stone to build a street of houses. At Hurst in Swaledale there are old workings which were

Ships built by the 'Geordies' of industrial Tyneside are known the world over. The nickname of these men echoes the renown of the great Newcastle engineer George Stephenson, one of whose early railway engines is preserved on Newcastle Station.

The great loop of the River Wear at Durham curves round a tall rock. On the rock are Durham Cathedral and Castle. The Cathedral guards the remains of St Cuthbert, who died in 687. The Castle of the Prince-bishops now houses part of Durham University.

'Coaly Tyne' has seen many changes since coals first began to be carried from Newcastle; but the years of depression between the two world wars diminished neither the skill of its workers nor its importance to British industry.

'Hadrian's Wall' from Tyne to Solway marked, save for outposts and occasional forays, the northernmost limit of the Roman Empire. North of it lie the historic battlefields of border warfare between Scots and English.

In that warfare the castles which the English built along the coast were invaluable. Here you see Bamburgh on its basalt rock, a Norman castle on a site fortified by the Saxons. Other such castles are Warkworth, Dunstanburgh, Alnwick.

A Norwegian or an Icelander will find himself at home among the place-names in these parts, which were settled by the Norsemen. High Force in Teesdale (above) will not surprise him, since he still calls a waterfall a 'foss.' The sheep, too, roam the fells, as they still roam *fjell* upon *fjell* in his own country

— and when the sheep are rounded up, the farmers can tell which are theirs by the ear-markings called 'lugs,' from the Old Scandinavian *lag*, a law. Norsemen and Celt mixed in the mountain regions, and the Cumbrian shepherd used to count his sheep with Celtic numerals, beginning 'Yan, tan, tether, mether, pimp . . .'

By comparison with the Alps or the Pyrenees, the Lakeland mountains are small, but diffusion of light through the clean, damp atmosphere often gives them an unsurpassed loveliness. This is Langdale after morning rain.

made by the Romans, and a tradition that the miners were British prisoners. A pig of Roman lead from the Hurst mine has been found and preserved; and we know that the monks in their turn smelted the ore in bell-pits, using the lead to roof their churches and abbeys, the silver for their altars.

Swaledale is a study in subdued colours: brown heights with rusty stretches of heather, until late August brings a riot of purple; brown becks fed by narrow grains growing like roots from the fells, stained with the peat, holding small bronze hump-backed trout; and brown narrow streets clinging to the heights, stringing the terraces, Keld, Thwaite, Muker; and Reeth drawing together Arkle and Swale, sitting at the point of the High Moors. Reeth was another market for the terrible knitters whose reputation stood so high that children were sent down from Kendal and the other Westmorland towns to learn the trade.

It is a country with an elemental simplicity. Take the road to Tan Hill and you will find the highest and perhaps the loneliest inn in all England. You may meet a shepherd or pass a peat digger, but that is all. Packmen and drovers were glad to call at Tan Hill, and it had a later heyday when the coalmines were working. Now there is nothing to see of man and his activities but the solid walls of the Inn, the bare road, and over the moors the stone pillars of the hill of Nine Standard Riggs (2,153 ft) marking the boundary between Yorkshire and Westmorland, dividing the bare wastes from the milk-and-honey slopes of the Eden Valley.

The lead and the coal have gone but the Norse lingers in the remote valley heads. Beck, wath, grain and tarn are Norse. Keld and Gunnerside were named by the Northmen – Keld named after a spring, while Gunnerside is Gunnar's shieling. The small cart is a coup, the hayloft a balk – the Durham miner still calls a heavy beam used for timbering underground a balk – a barn is a *laithe*, the senior workman on the farm a *hind*, and the two-year-old sheep a *gimmer*. These are only a few examples of a dialect that still stings with the Norse salt, and you are not surprised to hear that up to the early seventeenth century the common speech of the valley heads was more Scandinavian than English.

The hills of Cleveland are crowded and intimate, jostling together like molehills in the corner of a field, so low that you might mistake the waste-heaps of the ironstone mines for sister-hills, so small that a boy might start to run round one as he runs round a house in his village. The Danes left their mark here. At Roseberry Topping they worshipped Odin – its original name was Othenesberg. And at a distance the rockface scar near the summit looks like the rusted front of a Viking war-helmet, with the wings battered by the glancing blow of an elemental mace. From a distance – say, from that minnow-trap of a town Stokesley – the hills have a delectable cobwebby appearance. And now that the ironstone mining is receding to Eston, where the Clevelands have a last fling of the skirts at the furnaces of Middlesbrough, and to Skinningrove on the road to Whitby, where the unexpected furnaces outrage the sea, Nature is coming to her own again. There is a whole world to explore here, hidden valleys where small villages rub shoulders with the beehive dwellings of past races. And great moors running down to a coast of the North Sea that has not yet forgotten smuggling days, when Marske horses could make the journey to Stokesley unattended with a couple of barrels of brandy, and when every quayside inn and cottage had a cavity in the floor or a hidden cellar.

Now it is a coast the steelworker knows well for one holiday week in the year, with seaside resorts that grew with the railway and the steelworks; with a grand stretch of sand from Saltburn to Tees Mouth. From the mine-scarred hills you can look north to Middlesbrough, to the steelworks and the shipyards, to the sandy mouth of the Tees emerging from a wilderness of roof-tops, with the high towers and slung cables of the Transporter Bridge as a symbol of the energies of its people. Middlesbrough is a new, raw town, sprawling around its river and its industries, forgetful of Edward Pease, the Quaker, who brought the railway in 1830, and Henry Bölckow, the German iron master and first mayor of Middlesbrough, who exploited the nearby iron which caused the town's strange and sudden growth from the single house of 1820. Its speech is not coloured by Yorkshire or Durham. It speaks a flat lingo of its own fabricated in the docks, the shops and yards and beside the squat shapes of blast furnaces; looking to overseas for its lifeblood, and oblivious to the near hills which it has hollowed for its purposes, or the far away fells from which the Tees tumbles down.

And across the river, ravishing the coast, there are more work-shops to the north, more regimented suburbs, and the vast pipes and curved retorts of Billingham. The low sand-dunes interrupt all this only for a moment, and you come to Hartlepool and West Hartlepool as a last steel fist against the sea.

The great hall in Raby castle.

TEES TO TYNE

The stranger going by road to Newcastle passes through the shambles created by nearly a century and a half of rampant industrialism. He may have wondered why Durham County is so frequently omitted from the lists of County Guidebooks. After this journey he may understand only too well. The Great North Road and the main line of British Railways penetrate together the heart of the Durham coalfield. Leaving Darlington the traveller is woven through a monotonous landscape. The road cuts through the factory estate and new town which is growing like an inflammation around the old agricultural village of Aycliffe. Unlike Peterlee – the new town planned for East Durham and its expanding population – Aycliffe marks a complete re-orientation in the life of a community. It was on the northern flank of Brusselton Hill, which lies to the west of Aycliffe, that Stephenson laid the first rails of his Stockton and Darlington Railway. The railway opened out the South-west Durham coalfield. From 1825 to 1925 the measures were intensively worked. Strikes, depression, closing of pits and the inrush of vast quantities of water, together with uneconomic seams of coal, have contributed toward the decline. So the emphasis is moving from the coalfield to the factory. Light industries centred on smaller estates as at St Helen's, Bishop Auckland, Spennymoor and, on a larger scale, at Aycliffe are intended to pr vide a substitute for the declining industry.

Soon after Aycliffe is passed the road plunges into the coalfield. Everywhere are the headstocks of collieries. Smoke-stacks pour out a bilious reprisal of black, brown and yellow. The hawthorn hedges still surviving near colliery yards might have been cast in iron. Black desolate mountains of waste cut the skyline, and from the wrinkled slopes tufts of smoke and a dancing haze are evidence of the fires inside. Lakes of mud reflect the glow from batteries of coke-ovens; jumbled streets affront the eye. A mean and miserable architecture repeats itself – the homes of miners pitched impermanently on the heaving, ravaged earth. Sometimes there are long streets penetrating the guts of the pityard like tapeworms, with larger buildings like shabby boxes breaking their drab monotony. Amidst these the new sleek, well-designed pithead baths stand out oddly.

The chapels offer an escape. They are bare and devoid of ornamentation, although sometimes a false front makes a pathetic attempt to redeem the rest. Gloomy and smoke-grimed they are first cousins to the pit. In the dales the chapels are built solidly, sometimes nobly, of quarried stone. Here, with the pithead on the doorstep, the chapels are built like winding-houses or locomotive sheds. And yet, inside, the contrast can often be astonishing. Circular stairways wind to turret-pulpits where the preacher can stand like a captain before his people. Ascend to such a pulpit and even if you are no orator you feel a sense of power, for the pulpit is the centre of balance. The curved gallery, the rising tiers of pews, choir-stalls and organ all seem to draw in to the pulpit and preacher. The bare exterior may repel you, yet these raw bricks laid in mixed and mongrel styles are the symbol of a revolution. The bound men of the pits gathered eagerly around John Wesley, and Methodism became the established church of Durham. Methodism gave its strength to the struggle for a Miners' Union, and in early days many a branch was formed in the chapel vestry after the week-night prayer-meeting. The miner-Methodists were immensely practical men. They had little idea of architecture, but they often dug the foundations and laid the bricks themselves after working ten hard

Choir boys in procession in Durham Cathedral.

hours at the coalface. And they produced more enduring and noble monuments than their chapels in strong-hewn characters such as Peter Lee (after whom the new town is named), who was converted from a brawling drunken life almost in middle-age and rose to become chairman of the first Labour County Council in Britain and a leader of the Miners' Federation.

Beyond Neville's Cross – a grey mutilated stub is all that remains of the curiously fashioned Cross put up to commemorate the English victory over the Scots in 1347 – pits crowd the roadside and dominate the landscape. There is only a glimpse of Durham's Norman towers. The traveller threads an uneasy passage through pits and pit-villages. To the east the pseudo-doric Penshaw Monument surveys the plain. The road by-passes Chester-le-Street, where there was a Roman fort and where St Cuthbert's body rested awhile in a shrine before Durham Cathedral was built. East of the by-pass there is a welcome sight of grey stones folded in green – Lumley and Lambton Castles – Lambton of the Tyneside song and the fabled Worm, which grew and grew out of a well and ravaged the countryside and drank the cow's milk and was at last slain by John Lambton; the home, too, of 'Radical Jack,' John Lambton, first Earl of Durham (1792-1840), one of the framers of the Reform Bill. Lambton Castle stands a memorial to the wealth won underneath it. It dates from that great castle-building epoch between 1750 and 1850. Old castles like Alnwick and Brancepeth were built twice over in that period, at a cost of £250,000 each on the second occasion. Like Lowther and Beaufront, Lambton was a new castle, no 'Folly,' but a real castle built from coal royalties.

Just this oasis of green, then pits again lifting their high-peaked waste-heaps. Until at last comes Low Fell and Gateshead, with the planned factory estate of the Team Valley below, and Ravensworth Castle looking down from the far side on the smoke plumes of toy engines. The broad-beamed trams sway heavily through Gateshead, monopolizing the road. Then at last the meeting of many roads, the end of grimy streets in the wide opening of New Tyne Bridge, Newcastle. Beyond and below the bridge's severe beauty of curved steel lie the quaysides which the keelmen knew and the narrow, cobbled chares (streets) leading down to them. Down river the oily wash of waters between quayside warehouses, docks and slipways, with groups of slim cranes like fishing herons. Tugs, barges, tramps and steamers with flags of all nations. Upstream a vista of bridges – the low-level or swing-bridge, Robert Stephenson's High Level (1849) and the King Edward Bridge (1906). Under water now are the foundations of the bridge built by the Romans – and the old Tyne Bridge. Beneath the approach to the low-level, one of the arches of the old Tyne Bridge still exists. The narrow central part is the actual bridge built in 1248. Left of the New Bridge are the fragments of the castle which gave the city its name, the city of songs and singing speech, 'canny Newcassel'.

It is no provincial town, but a capital with great streets and distinctive buildings created by a speculative builder, Richard Grainger (1798-1861), from designs by John Dobson and John and Benjamin Green and others. Between the quays and the town wall are streets comparable with any, and fine individual buildings – the Central Station (1850), the Royal Arcade, the Theatre Royal and the covered market. But a city with more than meets the eye, for it has a speech, tradition and culture of its own, born of the early flowering of the Industrial Revolution. Spreading out from it are the industrial suburbs, products of a later unimaginative industrialism. But the folk who live in such suburbs still lean towards the centre. After Saturday's match they come down to the covered market; and the pantomime at the Theatre Royal is an annual event to look forward to. And every Sunday morning they get the bus to join the throng at Paddy's Market, where the stalls are set up in the shadow of great ships.

This, then, is the road to Newcastle. It is a good road in one sense: superficially it would seem that there is little to tempt the traveller to break his journey. The railway passes a hamlet known as Linger-and-die; the Great North Road a village called Pity Me. Both place-names would seem to sum up the prevailing atmosphere of Durham. But they do not. The collieries are a mask for pockets of beauty – Durham City with its cathedral, one of the noblest Romanesque buildings in Europe, of which I shall have more to say. There is lovely pastoral country, there are great stretches of moorland rising to the Cross Fell Range where Tees, Wear and South Tyne have their sources There are the long, narrow, heavily-wooded denes running inland from the East Durham coast – rare orchids like ladies' slipper, and the bee and fly orchids are no longer found in them, but at Castle Eden Dene the rare Argus butterfly still flutters. And just south of the industrial mouth of the Tyne, in a district frequented by holidaymakers from Tyneside, there is an unexpected colony of kittiwakes and fulmars on Marsden Rock.

The market towns such as Bishop Auckland and Houghton le Spring, both centres for the mining population, seem to live a double life. Miners and farming folk are alike at home in them. Houghton le Spring still remembers its beloved priest, Master Bernard Gilpin (1517-1583), that Apostle of the North who was not afraid to go preaching to the reivers of Rothbury. And Bishop Auckland with its Bishop's Palace has adjusted itself to the industrial epoch. Westwards are the great commons – once hunting forests for the Prince Bishops – seas of heather tumbling down to coal-mining country; and the lovely Derwent Valley, almost unknown below the cliffs of Consett slag.

Leave Barnard Castle and you are soon conscious of the naked basalt which has moulded Teesdale. The Tees below Barnard Castle breaks from its rocky bed to meander through conventionally picturesque but rich agricultural country. But above the town the river and becks reveal the terraced beds of mother-rock – the whin-dykes and sills of the lead-miners. The pillars of basalt break the smooth contours of the fells like elephant's legs. Nearing High Force you can look across to Holwick Fell where it drops suddenly in cliffs of basalt. Sometimes, by a trick of the light, this appears to be the edge of a vast forest, the front rank of a regiment of stone trees. At High Force the river has washed away the softer limestone and falls a hundred feet over basaltic bastions to the deep swirling pool below.

Follow the Alston road to Langdon Beck. There a road made for the lorries from the barytes mines winds to the summit of Widdybank Fell. Beside the old mine-shop you can park your car and half an hour's tramp will bring you to Caldron Snout. You have seen High Force. Now imagine a torrent 150 yards long with a total drop of 200 feet. The water flowing through miniature peat cliffs into the Weel, a natural dam, is constricted between stepped basaltic columns. The red wine of the peat is thrown through this series of cataracts; there is a continual cloud of spray and thundering of waters.

From the botanical point of view this is the most important place in the region. On Widdybank Fell, near the Snout, grows the spring gentian (which has a blue clearer and more illuminated than the blue of any other native flower), the bog-sandwort, a small, hairy-capsuled violet and the mealy primrose. Returning to High Force by the old track by Thistle Green over Cronkley Fell, you pass through a forest of juniper. The bare fell-top is a graveyard dotted with fallen tomb-stones of sugar-loaf limestone. You can look back and see Caldron Snout, a hand of white wool among the rocks, the river winding past the screes of Falcon Clints (the ravens are gone, but I have seen a peregrine falcon hawking above the screes), and the fold of the fells with whitewashed farms. As well as the grand spectacle of the fells there are smaller things to see – sphagnum mosses making a carpet of

A miner extending a duckbill loader conveyor, Ashington colliery, Northumberland.

garnet and Russian malachite, and lichens covering the rocks like a multitude of small precious stones. A pair of horns to mark the snow-bound deathbed of a Swaledale sheep, weathered bronze and green. And as you come to the heather again grouse rise, mouthing like little dogs, flying low, the red combs vivid against the fell.

Looking west you can see the dark shapes of mountains: the Cross Fell range, which gives birth to the great rivers. From Teesdale to the Tyne Gap is fell country, open, wild and free, with a bare grandeur of its own. The river valleys are thinly populated, but their people have an intense local patriotism, and if native ballads like *The Rookhope Ryde* are no longer sung in Weardale, there is still a dialect peculiar to this 20-mile stretch of valley. The well-dressed man is still 'weel put on,' the lad that falls goes 'tappy-lappy head ower heels,' the stout man is 'setten on,' the proud 'streck as a mennum' (straight as a minnow). And they still persist in saying contrariwise 'butter and bread' instead of 'bread and butter'. Beyond Wearhead are the mountain towns, Allanheads, Nenthead and Alston, where the corners of four counties meet, as if in conference. Beyond these, Hadrian's Wall, wandering 73 miles in oblivious old age, marks the end of distinctly Pennine scenery, the beginning of Northumbrian.

Squeezed between the North Sea, with the Baltic as its cultural tributary, and the Irish Sea, with its waterborne influences from the Atlantic and Mediterranean shores, it was inevitable that the North Country should be inhabited by the froth and jetsam of successive waves of migration. All left their mark on the land they lived in.

There were the 'pigmy flint' folk, who left as their tokens the tiny tools and hunting weapons found on the East Coast. There followed the various Neolithic races, earlier people who raised their monuments in stone – single stones, and stones in circles and rows – and who buried their dead in long barrows; later immigrants who buried their dead folded to fit into neat stone boxes – cists – placing with each a beaker, a knife, sometimes a jet or amber button, or a jet necklace. Still later immigrants brought the use of bronze, fashioning bronze swords, axes and knives, using gold instead of jet for personal adornment.

The Brythonic Celts came from the south and not from the sea. They brought naked iron, and may have introduced organized warfare. From them may have originated the local patriotism and zest for fighting which proved such an obstacle to the plans of Romans, Angles, Danes and Normans.

At some time during these periods (it may have been during the Bronze Age), the mysterious carvings on rocks and stones known as 'cup-and-ring marks' were made. They are found in north-eastern Northumberland and on the Yorkshire moors. Their commonest form is a hemispherical cavity, in some districts surrounded by from one to seven concentric grooves, sometimes interrupted by one straight groove leading out of the cup. There are many varieties, all made by pecking holes in the rock with a pointed tool and breaking down the spaces between the holes to form a line. But as to their meaning and purpose we know nothing at all.

Still later there were those who came as world-conquerors. But the Roman dominion was uneasy in Northumberland. Hadrian's Wall was built with the intention of keeping the area south of it free from disaffected Northumbrian tribes and from Caledonian invasion. In its final form it was of stone, eight feet thick, too high to be scaled by one man on another man's shoulders, and was protected by a ditch, from which it was separated by a narrow flat space or 'berm'. Within the wall ran a road and, some distance behind it, a great flat-bottomed

The gala day for miners in Durham.

ditch (the 'vallum'). The wall was pierced by fortified gateways about one mile apart, with watch-towers at intervals between them. It was further strengthened by strong fortresses like Housesteads.

Beyond the wall the Romans took their roads and forts, but it was none the less frontier country, uneasy territory. Sometimes the German or Iberian troops must have cast aside their gear to bathe in one of the lakes near the wall. A sentry sees the glimmer of white bodies in Craig Lough. The wind brings murmur of life from the settlement at Housesteads. Armour flashes in the sunlight and is gone. All that is left is the wall and vallum. Under the turf are houses and granaries, mills and aqueducts, tombs and temples; roots twine among rusting weapons and chain mail, crockery, coins and jewellery.

The years following the Roman withdrawal were dark and confused. The north, still culturally divided by the wall, was attacked in the west by the Irish. From the north came the Picts, from the east the Angles. By the beginning of the seventh century the Angles of Bernicia had complete control of what became later the kingdom of Northumbria. Pagans at first, they became converted to Christianity. Their wattle-and-daub houses have vanished, their most enduring monuments are their narrow churches. They may appear bare inside to us, but their severity of stonework was compensated inside by wall-paintings (of which traces can still be seen at Escombe, near Bishop Auckland), rich furnishings, screens of turned balusters (of which the *disjecta membra* can be seen at Jarrow and Monkwearmouth), ivory carvings, enamel and metalwork. And outside, carved, painted barge-boards and wrought-iron finials. The Anglian churches that we see now have been stripped of their warmth of furnishings and richness of colouring. We must imagine them as first built, the first flowerings of the faith that produced St Cuthbert and the Venerable Bede.

The Anglo-British style went out with the Scandinavian invasions of the ninth century. The new settlers left as their memorials the Norse crosses of Bewcastle; the fortress-churches of the Danes at Corbridge on the Tyne, Billingham by the Tees, Whittingham on the Aln. The churches of the Angles and Danes were never conceived in terms of bigness. They were built by, and meant for, small communities. Their builders knew little of architecture. At Escombe one can see how carefully they must have dismantled a Roman doorway at the nearby camp of Vinovia so as to rebuild it in exactly the same way.

The Normans, *per contra*, knew how to build and building was a passion with them. The small district churches they built in the Diocese of Durham (which included what is now the Diocese of Carlisle till the reign of Henry I) had each a nave twice as long as broad with a south doorway 11 feet from its west end, a square eastern sanctuary and an apse to the east of that. Two Escombes could have gone into the nearby Norman church of St Andrew's Auckland (South Church). But the tiny church of Escombe still retains a quality of homeliness, even with a derelict pit-heap tumbling almost to its porch, while the greater church seems alien and remote from its village, humped over the surrounding roofs like a watchdog.

The Normans did not believe in standardization. Tynemouth Priory, Carlisle Cathedral nave and Durham Cathedral are entirely different from each other in composition. The bishops gave their craftsmen plenty of scope. Durham, too, was influential abroad. Its ribbed, groined vaults preceded the 'ogival' Gothic vaults of France, and the saw-tooth gables made a greater impression on Germany and Scandinavia than in England, where they were so little liked that at a later date all the known examples, including Durham, were levelled off. Norman genius was not only expressed in churches. Masonry supplanted timber and earth for castles and house, and the Normans built such masterpieces of military architecture as the keeps of Carlisle, Norham, Bamburgh, Prudhoe, Newcastle and Richmond; and such noble halls as Puiset's in the castle of Durham.

The peaceful reign of Henry III brought prosperity and a sense of security to both sides of the Border, and this is reflected in the architecture of the period. Henry's reign gave the lower part of the choir of Carlisle, the Chapel of the Nine Altars at Durham, and the completion of the monasteries of Lanercost, Brinkburn, Newminster, Finchale, Tynemouth and Hexham. Guisborough, whose east gable is one of the grandest in England, and Egglestone Abbey were probably designed in Henry's reign. They have, particularly Egglestone, very interesting window tracery, the beginnings of that tremendous development which followed the discovery that leaded glass could be fixed direct into grooves in stonework. That development reached its highest point in the magnificent east window of Carlisle Cathedral – one of the largest in Britain.

The thirteenth and fourteenth centuries brought stone mansions, beautifully detailed, and unfortified, such as Hollinside, Haughton and Aydon. And private castles built under licence, many of them of great size and fine design. Lumley, Raby (illustrated on page 45), Ford, Chillingham, Naworth and Penrith are instances of these.

The Tudor contribution to northern architecture was the 'Bastle

House' or 'Strong House', which, with the already invented 'Peel Tower', became the only occupation of the local builders. These towers, like the earlier hill forts, form a constellation stretching through Northumberland and Cumberland. In Cumberland they were within signalling distance of each other. Later, mansions were built around some of these 'peels'.

The Union of the Crowns saw a boom in the building of those small stone manor houses with mullioned windows and debased Tudor details so common in the region. A Yorkshireman, Robert Trollope, brought variety of design in an effective Renaissance manner. But local styles developed, and the use of local materials, so to this day you can mark your passage through the different districts: grey stone in Northumberland, red in Cumberland, brown in Durham, slaty rubble in Westmorland and red bricks and pantiles on Tees-side.

THE CITY AND SHRINE OF ST CUTHBERT

Of all the works of man in the region the Norman cathedral of Durham is supreme, not only for mere bulk and mass, but for the enduring beauty of the stones which rise in monumental witness to the potency of St Cuthbert. It rises from its bed on a precipitous mass of rock concealed by plumes of trees. Almost encircled by the horse-shoe bend of the River Wear it is guarded to the north by the castle. The cathedral was the shrine of St Cuthbert, a stone box built to hold the incorruptible body of the saint. The Feretory, where his body was kept, has been described in that strangely moving and glittering book which was perhaps written by one of the last of the monks: 'exalted with the most curious workmanship, of fine and costly green marble, all limned and gilt with gold: having four seats or places convenient underneath for all the pilgrims or lame men to lean and rest on in the time of their offerings and prayers'. (*The Rites of Durham.*)

The fine sounding bells which rang to stir up all men's hearts when the cover of the shrine was raised, the lively images, the costly relics and jewels are all gone now, together with the King of Scotland's banner and Black Rood, taken at the Battle of Neville's Cross. But purged though the cathedral is of its glow of gold and glitter of jewels, we can still stand amazed at the supreme craftsmanship of ribbed vaulting half-lost in immense heights, of columnar piers and compound piers lifted in immobile procession.

The castle alongside was the seat of the prince-bishop of the County

A housewife in the colliery district of Newcastle hangs out her washing in the street

Palatinate. In him was vested almost sovereign power. He had his own courts of Chancery, Exchequer and Admiralty, and appointed chancellors, justices and sheriffs. He had the right to raise forces, levy subsidies, issue writs, and mint money. He could pardon the most serious crimes, grant pardons, hold parliaments and create Barons of the Palatinate. Bishop Bek rode to the Scottish wars with all the pomp and splendour of a prince: '. . . 26 standard bearers of his own household, and 140 knights formed his train; and 1,000 foot and 500 horse marched under the consecrated banner of St Cuthbert'. Knights waited upon him at table bare-headed, nobles addressed him on their knees. A far cry from the humble St Cuthbert of Farne with his dread of temporal power, hiding the comfortable gifts of his admirers and befriending the eider-duck.

Now the saint is almost forgotten. The growing university reminds us that the tradition of Bede is more in keeping with the present day. We have most of us come round to the way of thinking of the French Bishop who visited Durham just before the Dissolution. He offered a 'bawbee', the smallest of Scottish coins, to St Cuthbert, saying 'If thou art a Saint, pray for me', but at the shrine of Bede he offered a French crown, requesting his aid 'because he was a saint'. But for those of us who wish to re-create a vanished world there is a curious potency in the great bronze knocker which gave admittance to those seeking sanctuary. It is the mask of a demon set in a circlet of writhing petals. The eyes are round, fixed, and 'owl-like. From the mouth projects or hangs the ring of the knocker. It might well depict the face of one of those demons whom St Cuthbert found in possession of Holy Island. Or a mask of death, designed expressly that the fugitives who clung to it might see in the empty face the face of the murdered, or a fore-taste of the torments from which even the incorruptible body of the Saint could give no sanctuary. Nailed to the worn wood, it remains a curiosity for children to touch, a reminder of the porch which Wyatt destroyed a century and a half ago with its chambers above from which two monks kept continual watch night and day.

Around cathedral and castle are quiet Georgian streets in mellow curves, with narrow paths or 'vennels' leading down to green river walks. The houses and offices of university and church have porched doorways with shining brass door-knockers in a variety of shapes – dragons, horses, lions and unicorns. Some of the gates lead into secluded river-gardens which seem to have been especially created for perambulating scholars and dignitaries of the Church. The smoky plain with its pit-rows and pitheads seems remote from all this. But once every year there is a reminder of the smoking plains. The narrow streets from Framwellgate to Elvet fill with people. One by one representatives of every colliery in the county pass in procession. Each Lodge – or branch – marches under its own banner, and is 'played in' by its own band. The banners are great squares of silk depicting scenes from the history of the miners' struggle, or bearing portraits of their leaders. From some flutters a length of crêpe – a sign that one man who marched last year has fallen in action underground. As works of art these banners may be negligible, but their combined effect is hypnotic. The banners have a story to tell. Some have been carried from pits, where, standing on the heapstead, you can throw a piece of shale into the waters of Tyne. Others have come from the Derwent valley where heapsteads are hidden in green woods which Robert Surtees knew; or from the lower slopes of the Pennines where the timber is stacked on the moor, with snipe calling over bogs where the antlers of the great prehistoric deer are entangled with the roots of oak trees; and others from the coast where waste-tips have created new cliffs, landmarks for passing colliers. Into their fabric is woven a long history of struggle, a century and a half of strike, lockout and eviction, and the memory of the bound-men dressed in knee-breeches and white stockings, wearing posy waistcoats, and ear-rings to strengthen the eyesight.

The procession is not organized. There are no marshals, nor are any needed. Even during the ugly days of strike and depression the note of good humour was never lost. The banners are carried over the two twelfth-century bridges to the race-course where a great picnic takes place around the platforms. With the speeches over, the banners 'lift' once more and the outward procession begins. Now you will observe a change. The marchers of the morning came in marching four deep in almost military precision. The events of the day may have wrought a change. It may be the fluent speeches – or perhaps the crowded bars have an answer for it – but the folk go out dancing. Linked together in coach-and-horse style they sway below the banners. Gay in paper hats they shuttle to the throb of the brass bands. The banners are not so steady, as if they too would join in the carnival. The drummer sweats as his sticks swing in a dazzling arc and cornet-players, half-seas over, play like angels. Between banner and band the dancers sway happily; behind follow the raggle-taggle of family followers, and a thousand balloons lost in the thrust of the crowd float higher than the aloof towers of the cathedral.

NORTHUMBERLAND

That nakedness of the land which Sir Walter Scott commented upon nearly a century and a half ago still remains the chief feature of the Northumbrian landscape. The industrial population is concentrated

The housing estate at Scotswood-on-Tyne.

along the banks of the Tyne, thinning out towards Hexham, thickening towards the mouth of Tyne, with the wedge of coalfield tapering towards Amble. The rest is open country.

Where the Venerable Bede preached to the stones in the field is now a jungle of brick and steel; with workshops and slipways, the tall skeletons of ships imprisoned in high webs of scaffolding, masking the river. Grass-grown canyons mark where ship-yards died during the depression, silent epitaphs to unemployed and hunger-marchers. The priory of Tynemouth looks down on oily waters through which the squat Shields ferry makes its diagonal passage, a last link between the two banks and the twin towns. North and South Shields breed good sailors. Their native sons are born to talk of tales of ships and are coached in a tradition shaped by the keelmen. They see the ships building, they walk in the fish-markets supplied from the North Sea, Iceland and the Faroes. They see cargo boats from every port in the world, liners from Bergen and Oslo, a continual traffic of colliers, tankers, tugs and strings

The Team Valley Trading Estate at Durham.

of barges. They are not strange to foreign speech and ways. They know the Maltese, the Malays and Chinese of North Shields, and in the streets of South Shields they have mixed with an Arab population which possesses its own schools and mosques. Penned within a maze of mean streets the port and its quayside become their playground, and where we turn to the country to escape they turn to the sea.

Away from the river the land retains its nakedness. The industrial area carries 80 per cent of the population in an area less than one tenth of the whole. When the macabre fire-gutted hall of the gay Delavals (Seaton Delaval, built by Vanbrugh) and the conical pit-heaps of Blyth and Ashington recede, the traveller is in a land little changed since feudal times. There is nothing superfluous or lush about it. Since the basis of its agriculture is sheep and cattle-farming most of the fields are large, and the survival of the great landowning families has kept intact most of the great parks and country houses. The wild white cattle of Chillingham have had the freedom of six hundred acres of parkland for 700 years. They are truly wild, and if a young animal is handled by human beings the other members of the herd will kill it. They are the relics of a feudalism that has died hard, the living symbols of a tradition constantly menaced by moss-troopers from one side of the border or the other. This tradition gathered its strength from the great families: the Crasters, Widdringtons, Percies, Swinburnes and Fenwicks. Armed strength was their law, and their shepherds and farmers were also retainers, ready to take up arms at a moment's notice. Raids and counter-raids broke the monotony of brief periods of peace and gave constant practice for major invasions and massed battles.

What building there was during Norman and Tudor times was mainly confined to the castles and peel towers – so named because of the 'peel' or cattle enclosure which each possessed. Aeneas Silvius (later to become Pope Pius II) has left the record of a night spent in a border village; of how when darkness fell the men crowded into the tower, leaving the women and children outside to scurry into the woods when an alarm was given. Even in Elizabethan times visiting judges in the region of Newcastle were given a bodyguard, and the historian Camden was not able to venture far beyond Hadrian's wall for fear of Tynedale and Redesdale thieves. For it was not only intermittent warfare with the Scots that made life so unsettled south of the Border. The Wardens of the Marches had as much trouble with the quarrelsome clans of Redesdale, North Tyne and Coquetdale as with the men of the Lowlands. One unsuccessful raid by the men of Tyne as far south as Weardale is described in the ballad *Rookhope Ryde*.

Now all that remains to remind us of these times are crumbling peels, the great castles like Norham and Alnwick, the enduring names of families – and the ballads. As bare and simple as the environment which gave them birth they are the memorial of a folk who lived and died like savages. By our standards they were coarse, cruel, brutal. They were professional murderers, practised liars and ardent thieves. But they had the gift of song and they produced great poets. The ballads are concerned with the strong timber of life, with men and women, love, courage, chivalry and death. They were not written down, but remembered, and reshaped by many mouths; not meant to be read or recited but sung. 'I never heard the old song of Percy and Douglas,' wrote Sir Philip Sidney, 'that I found not my heart moved more than with a trumphet.' *The Battle of Otterburn, Chevy Chase, The Twa Corbies, Lady Maisry* and the *Lykewake Dirge* are full of that tragic but heroic quality which makes great poetry. Even read in cold print with the raw dialect as a bar to understanding, the faint whisper of Sidney's trumphet comes through. Benjamin Britten has set the *Lyke-wake Dirge* to music, and any reader who wishes to re-create the spirit of those times should listen to the recording of it made by Peter Pears.

The Union of the Crowns put an end to battles and ballad-making, though the local quarrels of the Tynedale and Redesdale men continued until late in the eighteenth century, while the ballad flared to a brief resurrection in the Jacobite period, notably in the *Lament of Derwentwater*. But the poetic genius of the Northumbrian survived in lyric songs like the brief and plaintive *Waters of Tyne*, *Blow the Wind Southerly*, and the *Bonny Fisher Lad*; and on Tyneside a native school of dialect poets grew into being with the immortal *Keel Row* and the *Bonny Pit Laddie*, and other songs like *Cushy Botterfield* which mark the decline to music-hall standards of humour:

> She's a big lass and a bonny lass,
> And she likes hor beor,
> They caal her Cushy Botterfield,
> An' a wish she was heor!

The ballads, the lyrical songs of the countryside and the humorous, sometimes hilarious songs of Tyneside have one thing in common. Their appeal is direct. They are unmistakably Northumbrian. They spring from that world which the wood engraver, Thomas Bewick, so minutely observed, a world in which the wind becomes almost visible; where rain and snow sweep bare moors. A world of low thorn hedges and stone-built houses with steeply-pitched roofs against a background of immense stretches of naked land and sky. In such an environment the solitary figures of men become precious, and we understand why Bewick brooded so long and with such care over a single feather, or saw so clearly the characteristic pose of a small animal or the turn of a twig.

SEA CASTLES AND BORDER FORTRESSES

Beyond Morpeth the Debatable Lands and the wild sea-castles beckon the traveller on. The Wansbeck valley with its country houses, Wallington outstanding among them, is quiet and prosperous. Morpeth, with a town hall designed by Vanbrugh, is the last of the coal-field towns. Beyond is Alnwick of Harry Hotspur, where the road narrows to pass through a gate-tower. The mute stone figures of soldiers on the battlements of the greatest of the border fortresses face the border, as does the lion with rigid tail which guards the Lion Bridge. Nearer to the coast is Warkworth Castle and the fourteenth-century bridge defended by a tower at the southern end. This is spacious country, with rivers, big with salmon and trout; Coquet, Tweed and Till. The Kyloe hills rise to the west, verdant and cobwebby, with the dour bald tops of the Cheviots beyond marking shepherds' country. Looking eastwards there are fragmentary islands in a skimmed-milk sea facing a coastline of sandy dunes broken by basaltic cliffs, with Dunstanburgh Castle like a jagged hand, Bamburgh a legendary castle on its rock, the 'Joyous Gard' of Malory.

Along this coastline hangs a continual fret of the sea, sometimes mere gossamer wisps of vapour, sometimes a slight sting on the cheek, often a bitter drive of rain like nails into the flesh. The great shell of Dunstanburgh stands empty and desolate, the masonry weathering to a union with the basalt upon which it is built, the tides savaging the broken rocks, rolling them like mere driftwood in the appropriately named narrow gorge of Rumble Churn. Dunstanburgh was fought for and fell five times during the Wars of the Roses and by the reign of Henry VIII was a ruin, after an active life of little more than 200 years. A short walk away is Dunstanstead, the birthplace of the medieval philosopher Duns Scotus – 'Of realty the rarest-veinèd unraveller.'

Bamburgh has a longer history. Ida, King of Bernicia built a fortress there, and it was for centuries the capital of Northumbria. It was the home of King Oswald, the patron of St Aidan. When the seat of government was removed to Corbridge in the eighth century it was held by the High Reeves and Sheriffs of Northumberland. It remained unconquered by Danes and Scots and survived the harrying of the Palatinate and Northumberland by William the Conqueror. The castle was bought by Lord Crewe, the last of the Prince Bishops, and in the school founded by him Grace Darling was educated. It is still occupied to this day.

From Seahouses, near Bamburgh, you can take a boat to the Farne Islands. St Cuthbert lived on the Inner Farne for eight years and re-turned there to die. He instituted one of the earliest attempts at bird-protection when he took the nesting eider duck under his care and imposed penalties on all who harmed them. Because of his association with the island it became a place of pilgrimage during the Middle

Pigeon fanciers – breeding pigeons is a favourite pastime among Durham and Northumberland miners.

Ages, and there are remains of the monastic house founded by the Convent of Durham. The eider duck – St Cuthbert's chicks – still nest beside the chapel named after him.

The Farnes are one of the most famous bird sanctuaries in the British Isles. Breeding birds include several thousand arctic terns, Sandwich terns (varying numbers from 300 pairs to 1,000 pairs in exceptional years), about a dozen pairs of roseate terns, up to 350 eider duck, and numbers of kittiwakes, guillemots, puffins and cormorants, with smaller numbers of shags, fulmar petrels, razorbills, ringed plovers and oyster-catchers. As the boat circles the Pinnacles, immense numbers of birds fly up from the flat tops of the perpendicular masses of basalt. The Farnes are the breeding station (the only one on the east coast) of the grey seal, and you can see the grotesque heads bobbing in the breaking waves around the Megstone.

Farther north, Holy Island, and the sands and mud-flats of the mainland, offer sanctuary to migrant birds, with over 200 species of winter-resident waders, seafowl and duck.

Berwick on Tweed is said to have stood more sieges than any town excepting Jersualem. It changed hands thirteen times during the border wars until its disputed nationality was settled by making it a county in its own right, though today it is part of Northumberland. It is a pleasant town to explore, with narrow cobbled streets, old houses and the oldest barracks in England, all within the town wall built by Edward I and strengthened by Elizabeth. The Tweed winds southward under the three bridges; the seventeenth-century bridge with fifteen beautifully rounded arches, Robert Stephenson's high railway viaduct, and the modern concrete bridge for motor traffic. A few miles upstream is Norham castle, massive walls rising sheer from the water, where Marmion rode out with his helm and crest of gold. Between Norham and Ford is the Duddo stone circle, the most perfect in Northumberland. The wide shallow waters of Tweed are joined by the waters of Till. Just above the meeting of the two rivers is the grand old bridge of Twizel, described by Leland as 'a stone bow, but greate and stronge', and farther up the Till valley the simple cross which marks the field of Flodden.

You can follow the Till towards its source, breaking away from it to visit Wooler. From there you can explore the Kyloes with their cup-and-ring marked stones, climb Cheviot (though, unlike Defoe, you will not be afraid of falling from the summit once you get there), Hedgehope and Yeavering Bell. There are stone circles, camps and peel towers and great tracts of bent grass, and hidden valleys with burns running ice-cold from the cellars of the hills. There are the immense folds of the hills, and the remote valleys of the moss-troopers, and the high moors above Rothbury and Otterburn. From Otterburn you can cross to the North Tyne and follow the twisting course of the North Tyne to Hadrian's Wall. Here you can walk on ancient stones and explore the old stations: Chesters, Housesteads, and Great Chesters, or the one town that existed in that strip of Northumberland south of the wall, Corstopitum (near Corbridge), with its temples to the gods of Gaul and Teuton, to Mithras and the more conventional Roman pantheon, with its granaries and workshops, its memories of exotic names of Legates and African Emperors, Syrian merchants and common soldiers from Holland, Spain and Hungary. Now their monuments are under turf or gathering dust in museums, and wall, vallum, forts and mile-castles are part and parcel of the countryside. But it is wonderful country. The wall loops over the bare hills where the vast shadows of monumental clouds continually pass in procession. It rides the rocky ridges from where you can see the glimmer of the North-umbrian loughs, hazards the Nine Nicks of Thirlwall and steep whinstone cliffs, rising and falling with the contour of the land through brown and green almost treeless country, to Cumberland and the Solway shore.

THE PICTURE TO-DAY

The theme which unites the two regions west and east of the barrier of the Pennines is coal. Steel is the strength of nations to-day where once it was corn, but coal, especially the coking coals in which these coalfields are so rich, is an essential in the making of steel. Coal gave birth to the industries of Tyneside, Teeside and west Cumberland. We owe a great deal to men like that Master Beaumont of whom Grey wrote in 1694 – 'A gentleman of ingenuity and rare parts, adventured into our mines with his £30,000; who brought with him many rare engines not known in these parts, as the art to bore with iron rods to try the deepnesse and thickness of the coale; rare engines to draw water out of the pits; wagons with one horse to carry down coales from the pits to the staithes. . . . Within a few years he consumed all his money, and rode home upon his light horse.' The art to bore with iron rods, and the introduction of machinery to drain the pits, opened out new possibilities in coalmining; but the idea of wagons and wagonways was the most potent of all. From the horse-drawn wagon running on wooden rails developed the railway worked by standing-engines. George Stephenson and Timothy Hackworth both worked on these early colliery railways, and between them made possible the expansion of the railway system and the use of the locomotive, opening out not only the 800 square miles of the North Eastern coalfield, but also the industrial potential of a nation, and eventually a whole world.

Between the wars the region began to show symptoms of an economic instability. In the early thirties unemployment became large, and it looked to many as though the great industrial empire was tottering. The shipbuilding industry and coal-mining were most affected, but iron, steel and engineering also suffered. In some localities as many as 70 per cent of the insured population was affected. West Cumberland, Northumberland and Durham lost thousands of people. These were the days of 'depressed areas', a term which concealed the misery and unrest of the major part of great masses of people.

The war brought a certain measure of relief. Trading Estates have since attracted new industries. But coalmining is moving to the coast and the underseas measures, and the inland collieries still existing have a limited expectation of life. There is much talk of re-grouping of population and of the creation of new towns in the North Eastern area. In Cumberland part of a long-term programme is to reduce the numbers of people living in the coalmining and iron-ore villages of the interior and rehouse them nearer the larger coastal towns. The development of an atomic energy station at Sellafield (Winscales) may help in the fulfilment of these plans.

Population is still increasing, and with it a demand for more roads, airports, new housing estates or new towns, which makes one fearful for the preservation of good farmland. The Lake District will soon become one of the first three National Parks and two more are proposed in the North, taking in the Roman Wall and the North York Moors. Conservation areas include the North Northumberland coast, with its many scenic and historic qualities.

The opportunity exists for a blending of urban and rural zones, and to reshape gradually and steadily that complex pattern which has arisen from the more or less sudden way in which industry has been superimposed on rurality.

There are few areas of Britain that offer such astonishing, sometimes violent contrasts, few with such a variety of men, of differing dialects and traditional skills. But however varied the local characteristics of the people they are all united in common pride of their north country. To understand that pride, to measure the quality of the folk, the reader must adventure into the region himself.

THE TOURS

Driving sheep from the fells to lower ground, near Ousby.

I F you cannot wander through the country at full leisure, the six tours described below should give you the essence of town and countryside with the least expenditure of time.

They have been prepared with the aid of local experts; and each of the six routes offers a comfortable day by car or coach; or a journey of two or three days if you are bicycling.

The routes are based on three centres – Penrith, Newcastle-upon-Tyne, and Durham. Any of these may equally well be chosen as a starting point for two of the tours; but to make reference easier they are numbered as though Penrith, had been chosen as the first centre. A map showing these will be found on the next page.

The tours are illustrated by special strip maps, somewhat after the style of road maps first made by John Ogilby (1600-1676) who called himself 'His Majesty's Cosmographer and Geographic Printer.' He produced the first comprehensive map of English roads.

The route is read from bottom to top of the page so that it can be followed as you go. The captions at the side indicate things of especial interest.

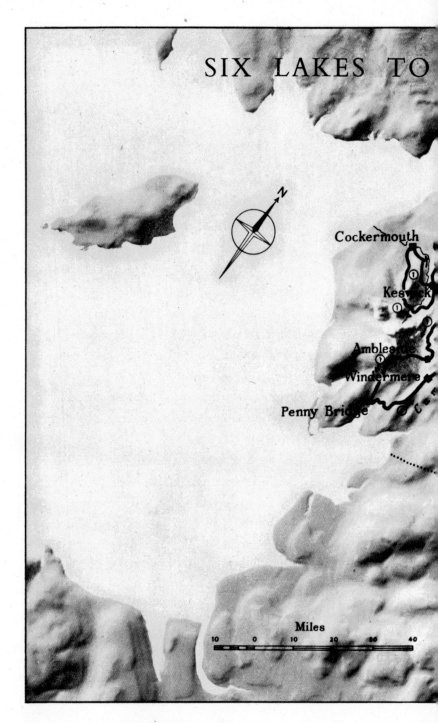

SIX LAKES TO

Cockermouth

Keswick

Ambleside

Windermere

Penny Bridge

Miles

10   0   10   20   30   40

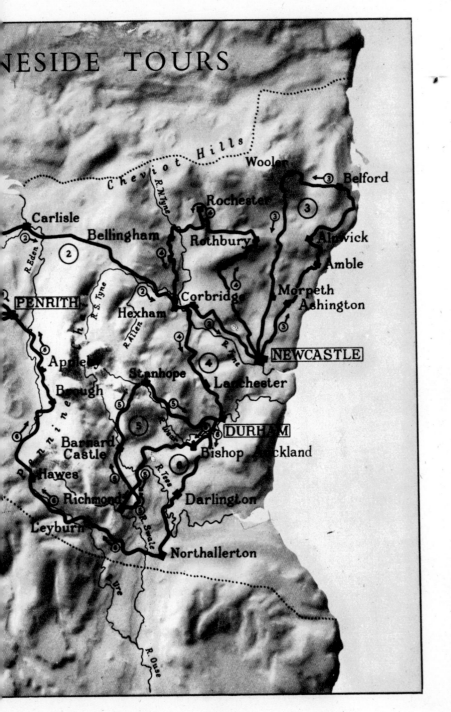

NESIDE TOURS

Tour 1
Penrith – Ambleside – Penrith.
120 miles

The Bowder (boulder) Stone is a large rock left stranded by a glacier.

Bowder Stone

Keswick. In Elizabethan times the ore was brought in to Keswick from mountain mines to be smelted – galena for lead and silver; copper was brought from Coniston.

Long Meg

Penrith is a sandstone town with narrow gulleys opening out to courts, and shops selling agricultural tools and implements – the real town behind the tourist façade.

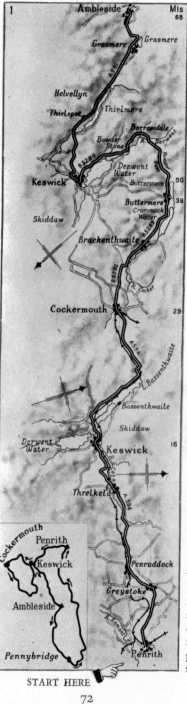

START HERE

There is a Guides' Race up and down a steep fell at Grasmere Sports.

Thirlmere and Helvellyn

Thirlspot is a starting point for the climb up Helvellyn.

Crummock Water and Buttermere were one lake until the silt poured in by becks gradually bridged them.

Cockermouth, gateway to and from the West Cumberland industrial coast, with its clogmakers and cattle-sales and the Cocker pouring like a millrace through the centre of the town.

The stone circle at Castlerigg is one of the three largest in the Lakes – 'Built by a people who made the rocks grow fingers' (Norman Nicholson). Most of them are volcanic rocks, although Long Meg at Little Salkeld is of sandstone.

White patches on the fellsides in summer are thick colonies of dog daisies – with regiments of foxgloves along the roadside.

Tour 1
concluded

Penrith is now an agricultural centre noted for its pedigree shorthorns. Penrith printers were once noted for their chap-books – some illustrated by Thomas Bewick – and Coleridge's 'Friend' was printed here.

Herds of the native red deer still wander in Martindale Deer Forest.

Windermere

Windermere: England's largest mere is the busiest of the lakes – with its regular steamship services, motor launches and racing yachts.

Thwaite Farm

Around Coniston Water, where John Ruskin lived and died, the Forestry Commission propose to extend their plantations.

Yanwath Hall

Yanwath Hall is a medieval semi-fortified building. At Eamont Bridge is King Arthur's Round Table, roughly 180 feet in diameter, with ditch, berm and outer rampart.

Near Bowness is St Martin's Church. In the glass of the E. window are the names and coats of arms of leading families of North Lancashire and Furness – among them the shield of the Washingtons of Warton, from whom George Washington was descended.

Beyond Pennybridge the road turns to follow the sandy Leven estuary which feeds into Morecambe Bay.

This lakeside landscape with its birch, hazel and wild cherry provided the background for Beatrix Potter's books for children. Thwaite Farm at the head of Coniston Water was owned by Miss Potter who bequeathed it to the National Trust.

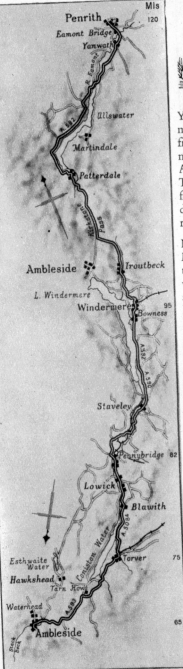

Mls
Penrith 120
Eamont Bridge
Yanwath
R. Eamont
A.592
Ullswater
Martindale
Patterdale
Kirkstone Pass
Ambleside
Troutbeck
L. Windermere
Windermere 95
Bowness
A.592
A.590
Staveley
Pennybridge 82
Lowick
Blawith
A.5084
Esthwaite Water
Coniston Water
Torver 75
Hawkshead
Tarn Hows
A.593
Waterhead 65
Stock Beck
Ambleside

Tour 2
Penrith – Brampton – Newcastle-on-Tyne.
100 miles

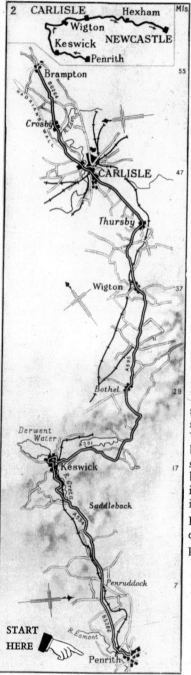

(map labels) 2 CARLISLE — Hexham — Wigton — NEWCASTLE — Keswick — Penrith — Mls — Brampton 55 — HADRIAN'S WALL — Crosby — R. Eden — CARLISLE 47 — Thursby — Wigton 37 — A595 — Bothel 29 — Derwent Water — A591 — Keswick 17 — R. Greta — Saddleback — A594 — Penruddock 7 — B5286 — START HERE — R. Eamont — Penrith

Carlisle. The Cathedral has suffered greatly. First from fire, then the destruction of the Reformers. During the Civil War most of the nave was pulled down to repair the city walls.

Wigton, where they make John Peel tweed, was once a Roman station. The sandstone church is built over the remains of the old abbey. It is in the centre of the Cumberland plain, and the sandstone used in building gives the soil around its warm red tint.

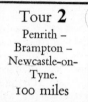

Keswick: Moot Hall

Penruddock
Note the dry walls. You may watch a waller at work and think there's nothing to it. But building drystone is an art. Each piece of stone must fit perfectly.

From Carlisle to Brampton the road runs parallel with Hadrian's Wall – place names like Walby, Wallhead and Oldwall are derived from their nearness to the Wall. Near Brampton is Castlesteads, a Roman fort.

Maryport

Away to the coast are the small drying ports like Silloth, and Maryport, and the sandy coastline of the Solway.

The Buzzard is a fairly common lakeland bird. An old bird sometimes has a wing span of over six feet. You can tell a buzzard by its long straight wings with blunted ends, and its call like the mewing of a kitten.

Keswick (see Gazetteer).

Penrith (see Gazetteer)

Penrith: Ancient Cross

The great suburbs of Newcastle stretch out monotonous arms of brick. But in spite of the suburbs Newcastle remains a community.

Corbridge : Vicarage

At Warden South and North Tyne join. Look at the map and you will see the old lead mines marked.

Beyond Bardon Mill the twin Allen rivers join the South Tyne, they come from the leadmining district of Allendale.

Thirlwall castle

It was to Brampton that Mayor and Corporation of Carlisle went to present the keys of the city to Prince Charles Edward.

B6318 follows the site of the Wall to Newcastle – Wades' road was constructed from the demolished stones, but odd sections are still preserved, and the vallum can be traced.

Corbridge: South of the Wall there are small unfortified settlements in addition to important settlement-forts like House-steads.

Hexham
(see Gazetteer)

Hexham: Flavius Monument

Haltwhistle: the Tipalt Burn runs through the real Tyne Gap and meets the South Tyne which runs almost due north from Alston.

Greenhead: Thirlwall Castle, Thirlwall Common: Thirl is derived from the 'thirling' or breaking through of Hadrian's Wall by the Picts.

75

Embleton: Nearest point to Craster, famous for its fighting family (a modern Craster is an authority on the bird life of the county), and its kippers.

Alnwick: Lion Gate

Coquet Island, a mile offshore, named from the river which enters the sea at Amble.

Bedlington: This solid, stone-built town was the capital of Bedlingtonshire; once a possession of the Palatinate of Durham.

Beyond Burradon Colliery the road crosses A190 which leads to Seaton Delaval Hall, built by Vanbrugh for the 'gay Delavals.'

Gosforth: Race meetings are held in the 800-acre park, the most outstanding being the Northumberland Plate.

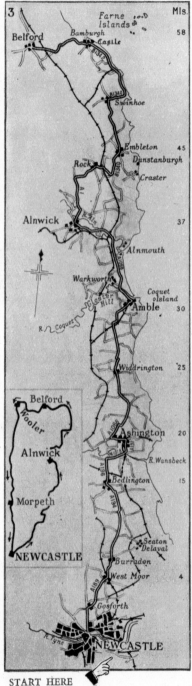

START HERE

Bamburgh

Bamburgh was the home of St Oswald and the ancient capital of Northumbria.

Where the road swings west to Alnwick, a fine view over the Alne, estuary of Alnmouth.

Warkworth: the small castle is featured in several scenes from both parts of Shakespeare's Henry IV.

Widdrington, the home of the knight of that name who fell at Chevy Chase.

Ashington has the longest colliery rows in Britain and a reputation for producing miners' leaders. The three pit heaps have taken fire, and smoke like volcanoes, fire by night and smoke by day – a landmark to passing ships.

Newcastle
(see Gazetteer)

Newcastle

The Great North Road passes through a mining area.

The busy centre of a mining district, Morpeth has Georgian brick houses, a town hall designed by Vanbrugh, and market-clock tower which was once a prison.

Harbottle Castle

Lilburn Tower is not a peel tower but a fine piece of Georgian Tudor by John Dobson. In Lilburn Church is the curiously carved monument to a medieval hunter. Anglers gather at Weldon Bridge – one of best stretches of the Coquet.

Near Chatton is Chillingham Castle and estate – home of the famous herd of wild cattle, of which less than a score survive. Both Bewick and Landseer had an uncomfortable time sketching them.

NEWCASTLE
Mls. 110
R. Tyne
Camperdown
R. Ouseburn
Seaton Burn
R. Blyth
Clifton
Morpeth
Castle 97
Mitford
R. Wansbeck
A697
Longhorsley
Coquet Dale
Weldon
Longframlington
THE DEVIL'S CAUSEWAY
Rothbury Forest
R. Breamish
Wooperton
Lilburn Tower
Chillingham Castle
Chatton
A697
A697
Cheviot Hills
Wooler 68
Kirknewton
R. Till
Belford 58

Cambo

Near Morpeth: Cambo, where Capability Brown went to school, home of the Northumbrian poet, Willie Robson.

The upper valley of the Coquet was another haunt of reivers. Harbottle Castle is in ruins, and the 16 peel towers surrounding it are gone. Cock-fighting mains were once held in this district. The Harbottle moors are rich in barrows and earthworks – and there is the Draag, or Druids, Stone.

Wooler is a good centre for exploring the Cheviots and Kyloes. There are cup-and-ring incised rocks in the Doddington area.

Near Wooler

On the Cheviot sheep-runs sheep are not counted to the acre, but acres to the sheep.

Rothbury: The medieval four-arched bridge over the Coquet has been reconstructed in concrete. Rothbury's castle was destroyed in the 19th century and its 14th-century rectory is now a children's home.

From Garleigh Moor there's a view worth stopping to see, of Rothbury beside the Coquet, the Simonside Hills to the west, and north-west the Cheviots.

wallington Hall

Newcastle United Football ground, the Barracks (early 19th century) and Leases Park – 'When Mayses breezes shake the treeses The cowses hooves go on the Leazes' – and Nuns Moor, separated from the Great Town Moor, and the Lesser Dukes Moor, by the grandstand – these form the green heart of modern New castle.

Visitors are welcomed at the Otterburn Woollen Mills where excellent tweeds, blankets, etc., are produced. The industry is traditional and women once took work away from the mills, using the cottage spinning wheel.

simonside

At Hartington the road turns sharply due east to catch the lower slopes of the Simonside Hills.

The grotesque figures overlooking the road keep guard over Wallington Hall. It was built by the Blacketts, a great Tyneside family of merchants and coal owners in the 18th century.

Belsay is a fine Italian arcaded village with a Grecian mansion, designed by Monck and John Dobson.

Newcastle

Along the valley are collieries with inter-connecting aerial ropeways spaced so infrequently that they do not spoil the effect of well-wooded pastoral land until Witton Gilbert and the more thickly populated area is reached.

colliery

The Tyne Valley widens below Hexham, with a fine view.

Hexham: Famed for its orchards and market gardens, the town is the best centre for exploring the Wall.

Low Brunton – Wall: between these two villages the road passes over Hadrian's Wall. Westwards is Cilernum (Chesters). The Redesdale Inn is the last in England on this route. These are the famous Debatable Lands of the border. Between Coquet and Rede is the Roman way of Agricola, later used as a reiving track, later still as a 'drift-way' by the Scots drovers.

Durham: Elvet Bridge

Durham (see gazetteer).

Shotley Bridge, now a suburb for the industrial town of Consett, was once a centre for flour milling, paper-works and cutlery-making.

R. Tyne near Hexham

Wark-on-Tyne is just another village, but when Tynedale was a possession of the Scottish King his courts of justice were held here.

Bellingham is a quiet village with a church of considerable interest.

R. Rede near Otterburn

Tour 5
Durham – Barnard Castle – Durham.
84 miles

Willington: its impressive flat-topped pithead is unique.

Frosterley: here were quarried the pillars of the Galilee or Lady Chapel, in Durham Cathedral.

Stanhope: the living was once one of the most lucrative in England – £8,000 a year. The Rector had his tithe of all the lead produced.

Richmond

Winston: the original bridge over the Tees, built in 1763, was said to be the largest arch in Europe at the time.

Bishop Auckland: the Bishop of Durham's Palace in its own park.

Spennymoor: one of the largest of Durham's mining towns. The Spennymoor Settlement has its own theatre, and a permanent collection of paintings by miner-artists.

Brancepeth Castle

Bedburn Castles: the road from Wolsingham to Hamsterley passes the prehistoric camp of 'The Castles.'

Egglestone (Durham): we take the moorland road to Stanhope, but the Teesdale road goes through to Middleton in Teesdale.

Barnard Castle to you, 'Barney' to its native sons. The market-town and capital of Teesdale proper.

Greta Bridge: the private golf-course of the Morritt Arms is on the earthworks of a Roman fort.

Staindrop : Raby Castle

Whitworth Hall: following a pleasant road with a fine avenue of trees approaches the home of the Bobbie Shafto who 'went to sea, silver buttons on his knee.'

Tour 6

Durham –
Leyburn –
Penrith.

104 miles

At Leeming Bar the route crosses the Great North Road – the stretch between Boroughbridge and Catterick was once notorious for its highwaymen and the innkeepers in league with them.

Beyond Croft the older houses are of mellow red brick in contrast to the grey of Durham limestone.

Darlington: Locomotive No.1

Once noted for the manufacture of linen, flax and worsted, Darlington is now a centre for heavy engineering. 'Locomotive No. 1,' the first that ever ran on a public railway, stands in Bank Top Station. (See Gazetteer.)

Durham Cathedral

Leyburn is the lower gateway of Wensleydale. Lead-mining ceased about 50 years ago; now the valley and its branches are famous for its flocks of sheep; Black-faced Swaledales from the fells; Wensleydales with long curly fleeces and blue faces, and cross-breds between the two – Mashams.

Northallerton gives its name to the old district of Allertonshire. From Bolton on Swale nearby hailed that 'poor old man,' Henry Jenkins, who lived to the age of 169, and remembered as a boy of ten or twelve taking a cartload of arrows to Northallerton to be used at Flodden Field.

coal landscape

Aycliffe Trading Estate was founded to provide an industrial centre for the derelict coalfield of S.W. Durham. There are many light industries, including plastics, clothing and light engineering.

Penrith. The town was founded by the Cambro-Celts. Like most lakeland towns it is built of local stone – in this case the Penrith Sandstone. (See gazetteer)

Appleby Market Place

Kirkby Stephen and Brough are better known on the East Coast than most of the Lakeland towns because they are on the main route to Blackpool.

The Quakers have played a great part in the development of Lakeland. George Fox visited Sedburgh in 1652.

The dale above Hawes is bleak, wide and wild; the farms few and far between.

The River Ure runs through a magnificent series of cascades between Aysgarth and Rodmire, known as Aysgarth Force.

Middleham Castle

Penrith Market Place

The Eden is one of the classical trout rivers of the North; otters flourish on fish and otter-hounds rarely fail to find a scent. The valley with its capital, Appleby, has the warm glow of sandstone country.

Kirkby Stephen: bound Satan in the Church

Hardraw Force, near Hawes, is the finest of the Wensleydale waterfalls. The water leaps over a ledge of stone 96 feet high.

Castle Bolton dwarfed by the massive square bulk of the castle in which Mary Queen of Scots was imprisoned.

Facing Leyburn, on the opposite side of the River Ure, is Middleham, famous for its racing stables and the Norman keep of its castle.

THE LAKES TO
TYNESIDE
GAZETTEER

BY H.G.STOKES

NOTE

This is a selective gazetteer of places and points of special interest or character – a topographical anthology. The numbers show the pages on which main references to these occur; bold type refers to illustrations.

For information about hotels, early closing days, markets, garages, etc., readers should refer to publications of the British Travel and Holidays Association, the British Hotels and Restaurants Association, the Royal Automobile Club, the Automobile Association or the Cyclists' Touring Club.

Many towns issue comprehensive lists of accommodation and guide booklets which can be obtained from the local Information Office. Further useful advice is also available in the area Holiday Guides published by British Railways.

ALLONBY, *Cumberland.*
Small seaside village on Solway Firth, with sand-shingle beach. Just outside the Lake District, but only 8 miles north-west of Cockermouth.

ALNWICK, *Northumberland.* 63.
Alnwick Castle, ancient home of the Percys, Custodians of the Border, stands some 30 miles from Berwick, where the Great North Road crosses the River Aln, near the walled town. Four miles south-east is Alnmouth, a quiet, unspoilt little seaside resort. Morpeth 16 m. S.

AMBLESIDE, *Westmorland.*
At an important road-crossing near the head of Windermere Lake (piers at Waterhead, ½ m. S.) with the curious Bridge House (National Trust) over the Stock Beck. Borrans Field (National Trust), between Ambleside and Waterhead, contains the remains of a Roman fort, relics from which are in the Armitt Library. Windermere 4 m. S.E.

APPLEBY, *Westmorland.*
To those who have crossed the fells by Brough, the descent into Appleby – trees, river and good stone houses – is particularly good. Here is a wide street of a market town, with Moot Hall and ancient crosses, and a ruined castle over it from among the trees. Penrith 12 m. N.W.

AYSGARTH, *Yorkshire.*
Wensleydale village with its picturesque waterfalls and home of Wensleydale cheese. Fishing, and a good centre for walking. The screen in the church is said to have come from Jervaulx Abbey (q.v.). Middleham 8 m. E.

AYTON, GREAT, *Yorkshire.*
The home of Captain Cook which formerly stood here has been taken to Australia and re-erected in Melbourne. He was born (1728) at Marton (4 m. N.W.) and is commemorated by a tall monument on Easby Moor (1,064 feet) – a mile south-east of Ayton.
Middlesbrough 7½ m. N.W.

BAINBRIDGE, *Yorkshire.*
In Wensleydale, where the river Bain comes down from the lake known as Semer Water and enters the village by a series of wide shallow falls. On a hill just west of Bainbridge the Romans had a fort: there is a small local collection of objects discovered there. Hawes 4 m. W.

BAMBURGH, *Northumberland.* **39,** 64.
The Norman castle (restored), built into a rock rising dramatically from the sandy shore, is open daily. The village is in peaceful contrast to this wind-battered spot, and the church has a good 13th-century crypt. Grace Darling is buried in the churchyard. Alnwick 13 m. S.

BARNARD CASTLE, *Yorkshire.*
Older than the ruined castle at the river-crossing (used by the Romans), and with great wide streets that bespeak its long history as a market town. Sheep are still brought to market, but wool has given way to leather as a local industry. It was at Barnard Castle that Dickens had the idea for *Master Humphrey's Clock*. Scott twice visited Rokeby Castle (south-east of the town) and described the local scenery in *Rokeby*. Bowes Museum, housed in a building in the style of a French Renaissance chateau, is a remarkable collection of pictures, furniture, costumes, etc. This we owe to John Bowes (1811-1885) and his wife (Mlle. Benoite), who collected most of the exhibits in France.
Darlington 15 m. E.

BARROW IN FURNESS, *Lancashire.* 13, **29.**
The town owes its rise to the discovery of rich deposits of hematite iron in the vicinity, though the steelworks and shipyards now use far more raw material than can be produced in Furness. This is the home of the great shipbuilding and engineering firm of Vickers-Armstrong. Off-shore the long narrow Walney Island shelters a good roadstead. North-east of the town, and in utter contrast to it, are the well-sited ruins of Furness Abbey. Rose-red walls of the church and chapter house stand, but the foundations of the whole establishment have been revealed.
Lancaster 18 m. S.E.

BASSENTHWAITE LAKE, *Cumberland.*
The most northern and least characteristic of the English Lakes. From the western side the twin summits of Skiddaw (3,059 feet) are well seen. Keswick 3½ m. S.E. of head of lake.

BEDALE, *Yorkshire.*
Old market town just off the Great North Road. Wide main street and a church with a massive tower and several noteworthy features. Bedale has ropeworks and the name is well known in hunting circles. Northallerton 7½ m. N.E.

BERWICK-ON-TWEED, *Northumberland.* 65.
Historic Border town with a curiously detached air that recalls its refusal to be included either in England or Scotland. Edwardian and Eliza-bethan town walls; remains of castle (most of which was demolished to make way for the railway station). Notable trio of bridges over the Tweed. Berwick ranks as a seaside resort with good sands. Famous for Tweed salmon fisheries. Wooler 16 m. S.

BISHOP AUCKLAND, *County Durham.* 50.
Market town and mining centre at point where the River Wear is joined by the Gaunless. The Bishops of Durham have had a residence here since the 12th century: their castle is a modern-ized 14th-century building. In recent years many new industries have been established in the neighbourhood, notably at Aycliffe, 6 m. S.E. Durham 9 m. N.E.

BORROWDALE, *Cumberland.*
The most beautiful of the Lake District valleys, much of it now protected from desecration by the National Trust. A lasting memorial to those who, by gifts of money or land, have enabled the Trust to preserve so many lovely and interesting places in the Lake District (its birthplace) and elsewhere. Keswick 3½-6 m. N.

BOWES, *Yorkshire.*
Bowes was the Roman Lavatrae, and the ruins of the Norman castle stand on the site of the Roman camp. Dickens stayed in the district while writing *Nicholas Nickleby*, and a house at the west end of the village is claimed as the original of Dotheboys Hall.
Barnard Castle 4 m. E.

BRANXTON, *Northumberland.*
A monument on a hill south-west of the village commemorates the Battle of Flodden (1513). Wooler 8 m. S.E.

BROUGH, *Westmorland.*
Compact village of stone-built, small-windowed houses. A haven for travellers when the wind batters the moors. Kirkby Stephen 4 m. S.

BUTTERMERE, *Cumberland.* **12.**
One of the smaller Lakeland centres, placed between the foot of Buttermere and the head of Crummock Water. South-eastward the road continues to Honister Pass – no longer the wild route up which only adventurous motorists could coax ordinary cars, though gradients still reach 1 in 4. Keswick 7 m. N.E.

CALDBECK, *Cumberland.*
Here was the home of that famous huntsman John Peel, and his grave is in the churchyard. Penrith 13 m. S.E.

CALDER ABBEY, *Cumberland.*
The few remains of a Norman abbey founded by monks from Furness (see Barrow in Furness) among trees beside the River Calder. Seascale 3 m. S.

84

CARLISLE, *Cumberland.*
A Border town astride the western route
between England and Scotland: it is also at the
western end of the Tyne Gap, and was the chief
station on the Roman Wall. There is a grim
red sandstone Norman castle; a cathedral, once
a monastic church, with good misericords. The
17th-century Tullie House is a county museum
and library. Railway works and biscuit making
are the principal industries. Carlisle is the centre
of a rich agricultural region, and its markets
are as much part of Cumberland as its castle.
   Penrith 17 m. S.E.

CARTER BAR, *Northumberland.*
At the summit of the Redesdale route into
Scotland. One of the most magnificent view-
points in England. Newcastle 47 m. S.E.

CARTMEL, *Lancashire.*
Quiet little town out of the main flow of Lake
District traffic and with a Priory church con-
taining some very fine wood carving and an
unusual tower. Windermere 12 m. N.

Hexham Abbey: Saxon Bishop's chair.

CATTERICK, *Yorkshire.*
In view of the size and importance of the
modern military camp here, it is worth noting
that the Romans also had a military camp here.
   Richmond 5 m. N.W.

CHESTER LE STREET, *County Durham.* 48.
Mining town on the Great North Road which
was the first resting-place of St Cuthbert (883).
The church is interesting for its 14 life-size
effigies, alleged to date from 1100, but mostly
of more recent date.
   East of the town is Lumley Castle (14th
century). Gateshead 7 m. N.

COCKERMOUTH, *Cumberland.*
An important road centre, the north-west portal
to the Lake District. Wordsworth was born
(1770) in a house in Main Street (open week-
days, except Thurs. National Trust).
   Keswick 10 m. S.E.

CONISTON, *Lancashire.* 11, 22.
Ruskin, for all his faults, was no mean judge of
scenery, as is proved by his decision to live at
Coniston. Brantwood, his house, is now a
Ruskin Museum, and his grave is in the church-
yard. One of the best ways of enjoying the
scenery is to take a boat on to the lake.
   Ambleside 6½ m. N.E.

CONSETT, *County Durham.*
Mining centre, with iron and steel works,
near the River Derwent. Durham 12 m. S.E.

CORBRIDGE, *Northumberland.* 66.
An important road junction and river crossing:
the remains of Roman *Corstopitum* indicate its
ancient strategic value. The Saxon tower of the
church has Roman material and also in the
churchyard is a 14th-century peel tower.
   Hexham 4 m. W.

DALTON IN FURNESS, *Lancashire.*
Birthplace of George Romney (1734-1802),
who is buried in the churchyard. In the market-
place is a curious (much restored) 14th-century
tower, once the courthouse of the lordship of
Dalton. Barrow in Furness 3½ m. S.W.

DARLINGTON, *County Durham.* 13, 45.
The development of railways is exemplified by
the contrast between Stephenson's first locomotive (1825), preserved at Bank Top Station,
and the great modern railway works which are
the main industry of the town.
   Middlesbrough 13 m. E.N.E.

DENT, *Yorkshire.*
Lovely little town squeezed into the narrow
valley of the River Dee. Birthplace (1785) of
Adam Sedgwick, the geologist.
   Sedbergh 4 m. N.W.

DERWENTWATER, *Cumberland.*
The most characteristic and, possibly, the most
beautiful of the English Lakes; of a size to give
proportion to the views from either shore, and
with a sufficiency of wooded islets to prevent
any suspicion of monotony. At its south end
is Borrowdale (q.v.). Keswick (q.v.) stands
near its north-east corner.

DUNSTANBURGH CASTLE, *Northumberland.* 64.
Strikingly situated on a rocky shore, almost as
described by Scott in *Marmion.*
   Alnwick 7 m. S.W.

DURHAM, *County Durham.* **36, 47, 53,** 55,
56, **61.**
The Norman cathedral originated in a Saxon
monastery built (in a tight loop of the River

Langdale Pike, Cumberland.

Wear) to provide a suitable resting place for the remains of St Cuthbert, which from 883-995 had been at Chester le Street (q.v.). The Norman castle was built as a protective work across the narrow neck of land. These two great buildings still rise supremely above the great industrial area of which Durham is the centre. The views from the riverside walks are magnificent and should be seen under changing conditions of light. The exterior of the cathedral has been badly 'restored,' but the interior is a wonderful exhibition of pure Norman work. Part of the castle is now used for residential purposes by Durham University; the Great Hall and the remains of the 14th-century chapel should be seen. Durham has a 16th-century Guildhall and a modern art gallery, but it appeals most as a city of steep, narrow, crowded streets, above which soar the towers of the cathedral. Newcastle 13 m. N.

EBCHESTER, *County Durham.*
Here was the Roman *Vindomora.* A pleasant little town on the River Derwent; the church has Roman stones. Gateshead 10 m. N.E.

EGTON, *Yorkshire.*
Egton is a plain-looking moorland village with a very attractive 'suburb', Egton Bridge, deep in the wooded valley of the Esk.
  Whitby 6½ m. E.N.E.

ELSDON, *Northumberland.*
A charming little village, well worth a visit, with its large green, its Norman mote and 15th-century rectory. Three and a half miles west is Otterburn, near which was fought a notable battle between the Percys and the Douglases (1388). Morpeth 17 m. S.E.

FARNE ISLANDS, *Northumberland.* **33,** 64.
A group of about 30 small islands (National Trust) famous as a breeding-place of birds – eider duck, fulmar petrel, kittiwake, tern, guillemot, etc. On the Inner Farne is a chapel associated with St Cuthbert. Grace Darling's father was keeper of the Longstone Lighthouse. Boats from Seahouses, 3 miles south-east of Bamburgh.

GATESHEAD, *County Durham.*
On the south bank of the Tyne, and joined to Newcastle by several bridges, of which the most notable is Robert Stephenson's High Level Bridge (1850). While staying in Gateshead Defoe wrote *Robinson Crusoe,* and here Thomas Bewick died.

GILSLAND, *Cumberland.*
Small spa (chalybeate waters) placed where the River Irthing comes down from the moors. Handy for the Roman Wall (q.v.).
  Haltwhistle 5 m. E.S.E.

86

Sheepdog trials at Barbon. Westmorland.

GOSFORTH, *Cumberland.*
Village on the seaward side of Ennerdale Fell, visited for the ancient cross (possibly 7th century) in the churchyard and the hog-backed and shrine-shaped tombstones.
Seascale 3 m. S.W.

GRANGE-OVER-SANDS, *Lancashire.*
Seaside resort on the estuary of the River Kent, at the northern end of Morecambe Bay. A good headquarters from which to explore southern Lake District. Kendal 11 m. N.E.

GRASMERE, *Westmorland.* **14, 18, 19.**
Here Wordsworth lived for some years and here he is buried beside his sister Mary and close to Hartley Coleridge. Dove Cottage (subsequently occupied by De Quincey) was his home from 1799-1808 and is now a museum of MSS., first editions and personal relics. Grasmere church is the scene of an annual rush-bearing. Attracting even greater crowds are the Grasmere Sports in August (wrestling, etc.).
Ambleside 3 m. S.E.

GUISBOROUGH, *Yorkshire.*
The beautiful ruined east end is all that remains of the priory which was once among the richest in Yorkshire. The town, too, has declined from the days when it was prosperous with mining alum and iron. Middlesbrough 8 m. N.W.

HALTWHISTLE, *Northumberland.*
Mining town among the moors at the point where the South Tyne takes an eastward course and is joined by the Caw. Two miles north is the Roman Wall (q.v.) and all around are Border castles. Hexham 13 m. E.

HARTLEPOOLS, THE, *County Durham.* 44.
Industrial centre and seaport comprising the original settlement of Hartlepool, on a limestone peninsula sheltering the extensive system of docks, and the more modern town of West Hartlepool. There was a religious settlement at Hartlepool as long ago as A.D. 640; St Hilda's Church (dating from 1190) is the oldest building in the town, but there are remains of the town walls.
Extensive sands south of the Hartlepools front the seaside resort of Seaton Carew.
Middlesbrough 8 m. S.

HAWES, *Yorkshire.*
Small stone-built town among the hills at the head of Wensleydale. One mile north-west is Hardraw Force, a waterfall 80 feet high; north of village is the Buttertubs Pass, named after the curious swallow-holes in the limestone.
Sedbergh 13 m. W.

HAWKSHEAD, *Lancashire.*
In appearance, at any rate, the most venerable of the Lakeland villages. Wordsworth attended the 16th-century grammar school. The Court House (half a mile north of village: National Trust) is a good pre-Reformation building, and the village contains many attractive cottages.
Ambleside 4 m. N.E.

HEXHAM, *Northumberland.* **85.**
Picturesque little town beautifully placed a few miles below the union of the North and South Tyne rivers. It was a Roman town, and the Abbey Church contains much Roman material and a very fine Roman tombstone. (Note also the pre-Norman bishop's chair, the 15th-century woodwork, and the inscribed cross.) Tyne Bridge is 13th century; the Moot Hall 15th century. Newcastle 20 m. E.

HOLY ISLAND (LINDISFARNE), *Northumberland.* **65.**
The monastery founded by Aidan in 634 and later associated with St Cuthbert was replaced by a Norman establishment of which the ruined church is the principal relic. The 16th-century castle was repaired and made habitable by Sir Edwin Lutyens (National Trust: open Thurs.). Holy Island shares the richly varied bird life of the Farne Island group (q.v.).
Bamburgh 5 m. S.E.

HOUGHTON LE SPRING, *County Durham.* **49.**
Colliery town with a modern industrial settlement and memories of Bernard Gilpin (1517-1583), 'the apostle of the North.' Finchale Priory is a pleasant group of ruins beside the River Wear.
Durham 6 m. S.W.

JARROW, *County Durham.*
A grim Tyneside shipbuilding centre, where stained glass was first made in England, and in the monastery the Venerable Bede (673-735) wrote his *Historia Ecclesiastica* (the church contains his chair and other relics).
Newcastle 5 m. W.

KENDAL, *Westmorland.*
A grey market town, centre of roads and fells, and the south-eastern portal to the Lake District. In the Norman castle Katherine Parr was born: it is now a ruin. The town retains many old buildings of the time when it was busy with wool and the church has chapels of the Parr and Strickland families. George Romney lived in Kendal for a time: some examples of his work are in the town hall.
Windermere 7 m. N.W.

KESWICK, *Cumberland.* **7,** 11.
Keswick's distinctive character is that of a comfortable market town with a very solid background; once the home of Coleridge, Shelley and Southey. Southey is buried in Crosthwaite churchyard. Hugh Walpole lived at the far end of Derwentwater, and there are some relics in the Keswick museum. The town is a good centre for exploring northern Lakeland, and there are boats of all kinds on Derwentwater and Bassenthwaite (q.v.). Ambleside 14 m. S.E.

KIRKBY LONSDALE, *Westmorland.*
Grey stone market town set high above one of the loveliest parts of the River Lune. Ruskin described its view as 'one of the loveliest in England, and therefore in the world.' The 'Devil's Bridge' over the Lune is probably 13th century, and the church has a Norman west door. The town is the 'Lowton' of *Jane Eyre*, Charlotte Brontë having been at school at Cowan Bridge (2 m. S.E.). Kendal 11 m. N.W.

KIRKBY STEPHEN, *Westmorland.*
Stone-built market town where the moorland roads descend to the upper valley of the River Eden, here fed by many lesser streams. The church has some reputedly Saxon work and in the Wharton chapel a curious carving of a rope-bound Satan. Appleby 9½ m. N.W.

KIRKNEWTON, *Northumberland.*
A village near the foot of Yeavering Bell (1,182 feet) commands fine views. The Cheviot (2,676 feet) is 5 miles south. The chancel and south transept of Kirknewton church are notable. Wooler 5 m. S.E.

LANERCOST, *Cumberland.*
Beside the River Irthing and just south of the Roman Wall (q.v.) are the remains of a 12th-century priory of which the church is still used.
Carlisle 10 m. S.W.

LEVENS HALL, *Westmorland.*
Elizabethan mansion famed for its park and its garden of clipped yews and evergreens. (Usually open on Thurs. afternoons from May-Nov.). About 2 miles north is Sizergh Castle.
Kendal 5 m. N.

LEYBURN, *Yorkshire.*
Small town on hillside with good views southward over Wensleydale. Popular resort for quiet holidays. Middleham 2 m. S.

LONGTOWN, *Cumberland.*
A Border town on the River Esk. West of the river was one of the last of the 'debatable lands.' The Border was finally marked by a dyke now contained in a plantation of conifers running westward from near Scotch Dyke Station. Carlisle 8 m. S.

MARYPORT, *Cumberland.*
Here the River Ellen enters the Solway Firth. There is a small harbour, from which coal is exported from the local mines, and a sandy beach. Cockermouth 7 m. S.E.

Newcastle Cathedral font.

MIDDLETON IN TEESDALE, *County Durham*.
A small town in Upper Teesdale. The waterfall of High Force (5 m. N.W.) is one of the finest in England.
Barnard Castle 9 m. S.E.

MORPETH, *Northumberland*.
Busy road centre and market town with some dignified Georgian buildings, and a church with interesting glass and ironwork.
Newcastle 14 m. S.

NEWBIGGIN BY THE SEA, *Northumberland*.
Popular seaside resort with fine sands. In a coal-mining area. Morpeth 8 m. W.

NEWCASTLE UPON TYNE, *Northumberland*. **35,** 48, **57, 89.**
Our great city of the North. Coals have been mined and exported from Newcastle at least since the 13th century; in modern times the deep waters of the Tyne have helped it to a high reputation as a port and shipbuilding centre, and there are numerous other industries. Much of the city is laid out on the high ground above the Tyne, and for all its industries there are some very good streets and buildings – including the cathedral, with its beautiful spire; castle, with 12th-century keep and 13th-century Black Gate (museum of Roman antiquities); Walker Art Gallery; Natural History Society Museum, and Library of Philosophical Society. Race meetings are held on the Town Moor.
Durham 13 m. S.

NORHAM, *Northumberland*. 66.
Border village dominated by the ruins of a Norman castle. The 12th-century church is worth seeing. Berwick 7 m. N.E.

NORTHALLERTON, *Yorkshire*.
Market town on the Great North Road as it passes between the Cleveland Hills and the West Yorkshire moorlands. The Battle of the Standard was fought 2½ miles north in 1138 (monument). Thirsk, 8 m. S.E.

NORTH SHIELDS, *Northumberland*.
Busy Tyneside port concerned with the export of coal. Now part of the borough of Tynemouth and linked by ferry with South Shields (q.v.). Birthplace of Victorian painter and illustrator M. Birket Foster (1825-1899).
Newcastle 7 m. S.W.

OVINGHAM, *Northumberland*.
In the churchyard is the grave of Thomas Bewick, naturalist and wood engraver (1753-1828), who was born at neighbouring Cherryburn. The village is sited beside the River Tyne where it begins to leave the industrialization of its lower reaches. Newcastle 9 m. E.

MIDDLESBROUGH, *Yorkshire*. 44.
Middlesbrough as we know it is almost entirely a development of the last hundred years, thanks to the proximity of the iron ore of the Cleveland hills. Here are some of the most important of English iron and steel works and there are extensive docks alongside the Tees estuary. Away from the iron works Middlesbrough reveals itself as a well-planned town with some good buildings and a museum.
Darlington 14 m. W.S.W.

PENRITH, *Cumberland.*
Sandstone town more akin to the bare fells southward than to the softer scenery of the Lake District, to which it is an important entry. Here are the ruins of a 14th-century castle, and in the churchyard the so-called Giant's Grave (15 feet long), bounded by two stones bearing pre-Norman carvings. Several historic sites are in the neighbourhood. Brougham (1½ m. S.E.) was the Roman *Brovacum* and has a castle which inspired Wordsworth to the *Song at the Feast of Brougham Castle.* Five miles south is Lowther Castle, the home of the Earl of Lonsdale.

Carlisle 17 m. N.W.

RAVENGLASS, *Cumberland.*
Village at the estuary formed by the Rivers Esk, Mite and Irt. At the foot of Eskdale, the best approach to Hardknott National Park (miniature railway as far as Boot). A mile east of the village is ruined Muncaster Castle and the remains of a Roman camp known as Walls Castle. By the coast is a gull sanctuary.

Gosforth 4½ m. N.

REDCAR, *Yorkshire.*
Seaside resort with extensive sands. Northward the Teesmouth breakwater stretches to sea.

Middlesbrough 8 m. S.W.

RICHMOND, *Yorkshire.* 33.
Market town on a steep hill crowned by the castle overlooking the River Swale. In the large market-place note how Holy Trinity Church is intermingled with shops. Nearby is the little Georgian Theatre where Garrick and Kean played. From the castle there are good views over the wooded river.

Northallerton 12 m. S.E.

ROMAN WALL, *Cumberland and Northumberland.* **13, 38,** 52.
Of all the Roman remains in Britain, Hadrian's Wall best illustrates the Roman genius for topography and for great constructional undertakings. The wall ran from Wallsend on the East Coast to Bowness on Solway Firth (73½ miles) and was accompanied by a vallum, or ditch, on the south side. Forts, mile-castles and other local works were incorporated. Many inscribed stones and monuments, etc., are in the museums at Chollerford and Housesteads, as well as at Newcastle and Carlisle.

ROSEBERRY TOPPING, *Yorkshire.*
The most worthwhile ascent of the Cleveland Hills on account of the fine views.

Guisborough 3 m. N.E.

ROTHBURY, *Northumberland.*
Beautifully situated grey stone village in Coquetdale. Excellent walking country, and north-westward many lanes wander in among the lower slopes of the Cheviots.

Morpeth 13 m. S.E.

RYDAL, *Cumberland.*
Rydal Water is small and delicately set among wooded slopes, while at Rydal Mount Wordsworth lived for 37 years and here he died in 1850. The cottage known as The Nab was successively occupied by De Quincey and by Hartley Coleridge. Ambleside 2 m. S.E.

ST BEES, *Cumberland.*
Sheltered by St Bees Head (rising 300 feet above the sea), and with sea-bathing, St Bees is also a good starting point for Lakeland fells either by Ennerdale or by Wastdale. St Bees School was founded 1587. The church, once monastic, has a Norman doorway.

Whitehaven 4 m. N.

SALTBURN BY THE SEA, *Yorkshire.*
Only 25 miles east of Darlington, Saltburn almost ranks as a seaside suburb. Certainly it is a popular resort of the iron-workers and their families. Only 3 miles south-east, though, is the busy iron-mining area including such places as Skelton and Skinningrove.

SEASCALE, *Cumberland.*
Small seaside resort with good sands and bathing and convenient access to Wastwater (7 m. E.). A good centre for sea-bathing and mountain walking. Egremont 6 m. N.

SEATON DELAVAL, *Northumberland.* 61.
Here is a partly ruined mansion which was one of Vanbrugh's most characteristic works. Seaton Sluice, on the coast 3 miles east, is a little forsaken port popular as a holiday resort.

Tynemouth 6 m. S.E.

SEDBERGH, *Yorkshire.*
Stone-built town of narrow, winding streets in the widening valley of the River Rawthay just above its junction with that of the Lune. The well-known school for boys dates from 1460. The church has some old work, but of more interest to many is the 16th-century Quaker meeting-house at Brigflatts, with memories of George Fox. Kendal 9 m. W.

SHAP, *Westmorland.*
Shap Summit (1,000 feet above the sea) is the highest point on the rail and road route between Penrith and the south. The village is bleakly situated, with the few remains of a Norman abbey, and there is good country westward. Shap Wells is 4 miles south-east on the east side of the main route: founded as a spa, but equally attractive these days as a centre for moorland walks. Penrith 9 m. N.

SILECROFT, *Cumberland.*
Small village near the coast and at the foot of Black Combe (1,969 feet), one of the finest viewpoints in England. Included on a clear day are Scotland, Wales, the Isle of Man, most of the Lakeland heights and a great extent of Yorkshire. Ulverston 10 m. E.S.E.

SILLOTH, *Cumberland.*
Small port trading principally with Ireland. Good bathing and good views of Criffel across the Firth. Carlisle 18 m. E.

SOUTH SHIELDS, *County Durham.* 60.
A great Tyneside port on the site of a Roman station of which remains have been excavated. Henry Greathead here perfected Lukin's design for a self-righting lifeboat (1790). Newcastle 8 m. W.

STAINDROP, *County Durham.*
The home of the Nevilles, whose monuments are in the church. Raby Castle has been described as 'the most perfect example of a 14th-century fortalice.' Bishop Auckland 8 m. N.E.

STAITHES, *Yorkshire.*
Picturesque fishing village beside a narrow cove in the cliffs. It is said that Captain Cook's ambition to become a sailor was implanted while he served as a shop assistant here. Sands at low tide.
  Whitby 9 m. S.E.

STOCKTON ON TEES, *Yorkshire.*
Between Stockton on Tees and Darlington was built (1821) the world's first steam-locomotive passenger railway. To-day Stockton is a busy port and shipbuilding centre. Darlington 10 m. W.S.W.

STOKESLEY, *Yorkshire.*
Once a flourishing market town, now quietly beautiful with its stone buildings and bridges over the little River Leven. Middlesbrough 7 m. N.

SUNDERLAND, *County Durham.*
Principal port of the Durham coalfields, placed at the deep-cut mouth of the River Wear. Numerous other industries have developed; glass-making has been practised locally since the hey-day of Monkwearmouth Priory, of which a few remains are incorporated in St Peter's church. Newcastle 10 m. N.W.

SWALEDALE, *Yorkshire.* 32, 33, 34.
From Richmond to Reeth (where Arkengarthdale comes in) the dale is buried in trees clinging to its steep rocky sides. Above Reeth the scene changes to an open pastoral valley, continuing thus by Gunnerside, Muker and Thwaite (where the Buttertubs Pass goes off to Hawes). 6 m. N. of Thwaite by a long climb is Tan Hill (1,732 feet), with one of the highest inns in England.

THIRLMERE, *Cumberland.*
A man-made lake which is the main source of domestic water for Manchester. Coniferous plantations hide the best views, but from the western shores there are glimpses of Helvellyn (3,118 feet) and Saddleback (2,847 feet). Keswick 4 m. N.W. from northern end.

Slaters Bridge, Little Langdale, Westmorland.

TYNEMOUTH, *Northumberland.*
Now a highly popular and progressive seaside resort, retaining many buildings from a more sedate age. From an earlier age still is the Priory, of which some beautiful remains are cared for by Ministry of Works. Public library has a notable collection of engravings.
  Newcastle 8 m. S.W.

ULLSWATER, *Westmorland.*
From S.W. of Penrith this beautiful lake winds in among the fells, with fine views of Helvellyn (W.) and of the High Street range (a Roman road ran over the top of it) southward. Much of the best scenery is now under protection of the National Trust.

ULVERSTON, *Lancashire.*
Small industrial town in Furness, on the outskirts of which is Swarthmoor Hall, where lived George Fox, the Quaker. The meeting house built (1688) by him is nearby.
  Barrow in Furness 8 m. S.W.

WALLSEND, *Northumberland.*
Tyneside town engaged in shipbuilding and engineering and glass-making. Here was the Roman Segedunum, at the eastern end of the Wall (q.v.). Newcastle 3 m. S.W.

WASTWATER, *Cumberland.* **9.**
Wildest and most remote of the Lakes, its inns and farms are the resort of climbers and walkers. Scafell Pike (3,210 feet) rises E. of the head of the lake and close to it is Esk Hause (2,984 feet), a great meeting place of mountain tracks from every direction. Wastwater with its weird screes and background of mountains is a lake apart from the rest.* Seascale 7 m. W.

WENSLEY, *Yorkshire.*
Very pretty village on River Ure – a good centre for exploring Wensleydale and the neighbouring moors.
Leyburn 1½ m. N.E.

WHITEHAVEN, *Cumberland.*
Notable for its submarine coal workings, extending 3 m. out from the coast. The coal is shipped from the harbour. Workington 7 m. N.

WHITLEY BAY, *Northumberland.*
Tyneside's most popular seaside resort. Good sands; ample amusements. North Shields 2 m. S.

WINDERMERE AND BOWNESS, *Westmorland.*
Windermere village sits above its lake and caters successfully for the enormous annual influx of visitors.
Bowness, down by the water's edge, is older (15th-century church has good ancient glass from Cartmel Priory) – a fascinating maze of wandering byways with a pier that constitutes the 'port' of Windermere lake. Kendal 7 m. S.E.

WINDERMERE LAKE, *Lancashire.*
Ten miles long and with an average width of about ¾ m., this is the largest as it is also the most popular sheet of water in the Lake District. Boats of all kinds ply for hire at Bowness, Ambleside and Newby Bridge, and from Bowness a ferry crosses to Sawrey on the western shore. The scenery is beautiful – low well-wooded hills with distant views of the higher fells.

WOOLER, *Northumberland.* **66.**
Nicely situated town on the edge of the Cheviots: good centre for excursions.
Alnwick 14 m. S.E.

WORKINGTON, *Cumberland.*
Here the River Derwent ends its lovely course through Borrowdale, Derwentwater, Bassenthwaite, and the pastoral country along by Cockermouth. The interests of Workington are coal, iron and chemicals. Whitehaven 7 m. S.

YARM, *Yorkshire.*
In a loop of the River Tees where it is crossed by road and railway, and with a wide main street bespeaking a long succession of markets and fairs. Stockton-on-Tees 4 m. N.